Life in the
English Country
Cottage

Life in the English Country Cottage

ADRIAN TINNISWOOD

Weidenfeld & Nicolson

London

Text © Adrian Tinniswood
Book © Weidenfeld & Nicolson

First published in 1995 by
George Weidenfeld & Nicolson Limited
The Orion Publishing Group
Orion House
5 Upper St Martin's Lane
London WC2H 9EA

British Library Cataloguing-in-Publication Data
A record for this book is available from the British Library

ISBN 0 297 83274 3

Project Editor: Phyllis Richardson
Designed by the Bridgewater Book Company
Printed and bound in Italy

ENDPAPERS
Six Cottages at Elmsthorpe near Leicester,
by Charles F. A. Voysey.

HALF-TITLE PAGE
Pedlar at a Cottage Door, Dorset,
from the collection of Thomas Hardy.

TITLE FRONTISPIECE
A Cottage Doorway, by William Egerton Hine.

CONTENTS FRONTISPIECE
Landscape with Cottages, by William Mulready.

For Ciara and Lauren

ACKNOWLEDGMENTS

Many people have helped in the production of this book. My thanks to them all, and especially to Anthony Beeson, Iain Osborn, Gareth Binns, John Hodgson, Lucas Dietrich, Phyllis Richardson and Helen.

CONTENTS

Hearth and Home

*Contrast these old houses with the modern suburban abominations, 'those
thin tottering foundationless shells of splintered wood and imitated stone',
those gloomy rows of formalised minuteness, alike without difference and
without fellowship, as solitary as similar', as Ruskin calls them . . . Age
cannot improve the appearance of such things. But age only mellows and
improves our ancient houses. Solidly built of good materials, the golden
stain of time only adds to their beauties . . . and the passing of the centuries
has served but to tone them down and bring them into closer harmony
with nature.*

P. H. DITCHFIELD, *VANISHING ENGLAND*, 1910

In 1927 the AMA Portable and Permanent Building Works marketed a popular single-storey cottage that made use of a timber frame clad in asbestos cement sheets, with weatherboarding up to the height of the window sills. The roof-covering consisted of diamond-pattern asbestos tiles 'available in various colours'. Intended for chauffeur, gardener, weekend or general use, the whole thing was perfectly hideous. It was called 'My Heart's Desire'.

The irony of that name epitomizes a great deal of twentieth-century thinking about the cottage as a place to live in. The country cottage has indeed become an object of desire, a pot of gold at the end of the rainbow. It is an icon for the 1990s, signifying a better, safer, quieter life away from the city, a potent focus for the anti-urbanism that looms so large in modern thought.

The very word 'cottage' conjures up a whole host of cosy meanings. One only has to glance through the *Yellow Pages* to find among the Cottage Bakeries and Cottage Tea Rooms, with their comfortable pre-war associations with the world of Miss Marple or Mapp and Lucia, increasingly bizarre juxtapositions – the Cottage Caravan Park, Cottage Design and Print, even Cottage Fish and Chips. The cottage hospital, where it still survives, reassures us with a friendlier, less frightening approach to sickness and death than the echoing labyrinthine corridors and impersonal wards of the general hospital. The telecottage softens the hard edge of technology by seeking to locate the personal computers, faxes and modems in a homely rural setting.

The contemporary notion of the country cottage is a long way from 'My Heart's Desire', with its cement sheets and asbestos tiles. The promise of sanctuary that it carries has a more positive side that suggests 'escape to' as well as 'escape from'. Few real cottages conform to the clichés of

THE LODGE TO
WOLLSTON HOUSE,
BUILT *c*. 1830–50, IN
LODDISWELL, DEVON.

deep overhanging thatch and roses round the door. But their rural setting, their irregular outlines, their adherence to local traditions and building styles, all evoke country living, easy access to the rural landscape, a sense of belonging to a small, tightknit community. More importantly, they suggest associations with an organic natural growth, centuries of continuity and change that have made them what they are today.

But to what extent does this rosy picture of the English country cottage conform to the reality of life for the cottager and his family in the past? That question is a thread that runs through the whole of this book, but in order to answer it one has first to grapple with a basic problem of definition. What exactly is meant by the word 'cottage'? And what did people mean by it in the past?

Dr Johnson's classic definition of a cottage was characteristically uncompromising – 'a mean habitation'. Dr Watts agreed, but located it firmly in a rural setting, saying it

A PICTURESQUE THATCHTED COTTAGE, BUILT *c.*1840, IN BADMINTON, AVON.

was 'a mean house in the country'. Modern dictionaries tend to emphasize size rather than housing standards: 'a labourer's or villager's small dwelling'; 'a small country or suburban house'. But already the alarm bells start to ring – how small is small? Come to that, how mean is mean?

Not all that mean, and not all that small either, if the Devon cottage that the Dashwoods retire to in Jane Austen's *Sense and Sensibility* is anything to go by. Barton Cottage has four bedrooms, a garden and accommodation for servants in the attic. Even so, Mrs Dashwood doesn't like it:

As a cottage it was defective, for the building was regular, the roof was tiled, the window shutters were not painted green, nor were the walls covered with honeysuckles. A narrow passage led directly through the house into the garden behind. On each side of the entrance was a sitting room, about sixteen feet square; and beyond them were the offices and stairs.

Jane Austen was writing *Sense and Sensibility* between the years 1797 and 1811, a time when the gentrification of the

English cottage was gathering a momentum that has carried through into the late twentieth century. If we really want to see small and mean, however, we can compare Austen's account with a roughly contemporary picture by the travel-writer William Hutchinson of cottages in Northumberland:

> *The cottages of the lower class of people are deplorable, composed of upright timbers fixed in the ground, the interstices wattled and plastered with mud; the roofs, some thatched and others covered with turf; one little piece of glass to admit the beams of day; and a hearthstone on the ground, for the peat and turf fire. Within there was a scene to touch the feelings of the heart . . . the damp earth, the naked rafters, the breeze-disturbed embers . . . the midday gloom, the wretched couch, the wooden utensils that scarce retain the name of convenience, the domestic beast that stalls with his master, the disconsolate poultry that mourns upon the rafters, form a group of objects suitable for a great man's contemplation.*

POSTWAR LIFE IN THE ENGLISH COUNTRY COTTAGE. SALTHOUSE, NORFOLK, 1953.

DESIGNS FROM J. C. LOUDON'S *FORMING, IMPROVING AND MANAGING COUNTRY RESIDENCES*, 1806.

It is quite a broad definition that can take in Barton Cottage, with its servants' quarters, four bedrooms and two good-sized reception rooms (one of which, incidentally, houses Miss Dashwood's piano); and a Northumberland labourer's home which is little more than a hut. The latter is probably no bigger in its entirety than one of the Dashwoods' sitting rooms and features hens in the rafters, earth floors and a cow standing in for the piano. Both, however, are authentic portrayals of cottage life in late-Georgian England, and they indicate just how loosely the term was – and still is – interpreted.

The large, double-fronted house in *Sense and Sensibility* looks forward to twentieth-century ideas of the cottage, while the squalid hovels of

Northumberland look back to its origins. The housing conditions of those labourers and their families on the Borders (admittedly what was then an area of the country notorious for its poor housing), had a great deal in common with life in the homes of our forebears. The poorer medieval peasant also shared his cottage with the livestock. He, too, lived in a single-room house with bare floors and few conveniences beyond a fire and a roof. The only real difference was that a piece of wood or sacking would have taken the place of the 'one little piece of glass to admit the beams of day'.

We have forgotten what life in the English cottage was really like for most rural labourers, not just in the Middle Ages, but right up into the late nineteenth century. They were the poorest members of society. Their houses were generally small, cramped, ill-equipped and badly built, so badly built, in fact, that they were apt to fall down at the drop of a hat. Witness the case of the two-month-old Norfolk baby who was killed on Christmas Day 1362 when a partition-wall fell on him without warning as he lay in his mother's bed. No one in their right mind would live in a cottage from choice.

The thatch-and-roses image of cottage life is a relatively recent construct. It belongs to an educated urban middle class, and like our love of the countryside itself, it is a conse-quence of an Industrial Revolution that drew most of the population away from that coun-

THE RAISING OF LIVESTOCK WAS AN IMPORTANT PART OF THE COTTAGERS' ECONOMY.

tryside and deposited them in towns and cities where they could happily mythologize their rural roots. That is not to dismiss the very real appeal of the country cottage. If this analysis sounds like a fashionable and rather tired sneer at the Volvo-and-green-wellingtons brigade, forcing up house prices and patronizing the locals, it is not meant to. (Such an attitude would be unpardonable hypocrisy on the part of someone who left the suburbs for a West Country cottage ten years ago.) But it is important to remember that with the cottage, as with all things, we remake the past, and in remaking it we leave out an awful lot.

Like all architecture, cottages are first and foremost expressions of human behaviour. The key to understanding them lies in appreciating how people regarded them at various times in history, what people did in them, and the relationships that the people who lived in them had with the rest of society. That is what this book is about. But most important of all – and hardest of all to achieve – is to comprehend cottagers as individuals.

A coroner's roll tells us that one Tuesday night in April 1322, while Robert and Matilda and their two sons, William and John, lay asleep, 'a lighted candle fixed on the wall by the said Matilda fell by accident on the bed of the said Robert and Matilda and set the whole house on fire; that the said Robert and William were immediately caught in the flames and burnt and Matilda and John with difficulty escaped with their lives'. Another coroner's roll describes how on 9 August 1298, John Trivaler and his wife Alice were woken

ENCLOSED FIREPLACES WITH CHIMNIES WERE NOT COMMON IN COTTAGES UNTIL THE LATE 16TH CENTURY.

by a fire, again caused by a lighted candle. They rushed from their house, only to realize that their child was still inside, 'And immediately when the said Alice remembered her son was in the fire within, she leaped back . . . to seek him, and immediately when she entered she was overcome by the greatness of the fire and choked.' In 1581 Margaret Matheson of Foxton in Cambridgeshire, sick with the plague, made her last will and testament:

She havinge twoe of her children ded of the plague & lyeinge unburyed, and haveinge two other children verye sicke & she her selfe beinge sicke of the same decease, did give all her goodes that she had what soever unto Ralph Wade and Margary his wife, sister of the sayd Margaret Matheson, to burye her and her said children.

Such glimpses into the tragedies that afflicted ordinary lives remind us that no lives are ordinary. The history books tell us that in 1298 Edward I defeated Wallace at the Battle of Stirling; what did that matter to John Trivaler, trying to cope with the loss of his wife and only child? Elizabeth I may have been knighting Sir Francis Drake aboard the *Golden Hind* in 1581, but the event seems trivial compared to Margaret Matheson's stoic suffering as she lay on her deathbed worrying about her unburied children.

The old English country cottage is not just a nice place to live, or a money-pit, depending on how lucky or dedicated you are. Nor is it simply a focus for recondite research into plan-forms, construction methods and dendrochronology, interesting and valuable though that may be. It is a monument to the people who lived in it. Even if we do not know their names, we know their homes, and that in itself is a form of acquaintance.

In 1899 H. Rider Haggard came across an old cottage at Bedingham in Norfolk. The thoughts that cottage provoked comprise a convenient summary for the reasons behind the writing of this book:

Oh! if only the place could tell all its story, with the detail necessary to make us understand it, what a story that would be! A humble tale perhaps – a tale of little things and obscure lives and yet how fascinating! When we consider bygone ages we are apt to dwell only upon the histories of distinguished individuals and the records of great and startling occurrences. Yet those do not really make up the past.

A GROUP OF RURAL ENGLISH VILLAGERS IN THE 1930S.

Notable men are rare; there be very few in any age who can lift their heads and voices high enough above the raving crowd for the world to see and hear them, and great events occur only from time to time. But behind these Titans existed the dim multitudes of the people – those whose qualities and characters really fashioned the nation for good or ill; our forefathers, whose instincts and strivings built up the empire we inherit, in whom lay the weight and influence which brought about the revolutions in our history . . . But of all these forgotten humble hordes there remains nothing but ourselves, who, by the mysterious descent of blood, continue their existence, and such poor memorials as are inscribed by some long-dead hand upon the imperishable stone.

CHAPTER I

To The
Manor Born
1066-1500

William Couper, who held a cottage and 4 acres of bondage land there [in the manor of Bradford, Yorks.], is dead; and hereupon came Roger, his son and heir, and took those tenements, to hold to him and his heirs according to the custom of the manor.

COURT ROLLS OF THE MANOR OF BRADFORD, 12 DECEMBER 1349

In 1125 the village of Pytchley, a few miles southwest of Kettering in Northamptonshire, consisted of thirty-seven men and their families. Most were bonded men, owing certain dues to their lord, the Abbey of Peterborough. Among this latter group there were nine villeins, nine half-villeins, and five cottars or cottagers. For most of the year the full villeins worked three days a week on their lord's lands. They also worked every day of the week from the middle of August to Michaelmas, 29 September, which was the busiest time of the agricultural year, when the harvest was being gathered. The half-villeins worked 'in accordance with their tenures', and the cottagers one day a week, and two in August.

Each full villein was expected to plough and harrow one acre at the winter ploughing and one at the spring, and to winnow the seed in the lord's grange and sow it. The half-villeins had to lend their plough teams three times at the winter ploughing, three times at the spring ploughing and once for harrowing, 'and what they plough they reap and cart'. Between them the bondsmen could muster eight plough-teams. In addition to being obliged to provide direct labour for their lord, they were expected to pay him five

AN 11TH-CENTURY CALENDAR ILLUSTRATION SHOWS THE PLIGHT OF

PEASANTS WORKING IN THE FIELDS – THEIR LORD'S AND THEIR OWN.

shillings at Christmas, five shillings at Easter and thirty-two pence when they began work on the harvest. There were also payments in kind: all the villeins had to hand over thirty-two hens at Christmas, while at Easter the full villeins gave twenty eggs, the half-villeins ten eggs and the cottars five eggs.

The twelfth-century survey of Peterborough Abbey's estates from which this information comes also tells us that besides these unnamed bonded tenants, whose tenure depended on their giving service and various dues in return for their holdings, there were thirteen freemen renting land at Pytchley from the Abbey. (A fourteenth was a 'sokeman', that is, his land was his own but he still had to pay certain dues to the lord of the manor.) The village smith, Leofric, paid twelve pence for his smithy and the cottage that went with it. Agemund the miller paid twenty-six shillings for his mill and one virgate, while the parish priest paid five shillings for the church and two virgates. A virgate was the amount of land held by a full villein. Scattered in strips over the common fields,it was usually reckoned to be around thirty acres, but in practice it varied as much as fifty per cent either way from one part of the country to another. Half-villeins held roughly half a virgate.

Other freemen paid different amounts of rent. 'Viel renders three shillings for one virgate and Aze five . . . Aegelric of Kettering pays six pence for the land he rents and Aegelric of Broughton twelve pence and Lambert twelve pence.' At the bottom of the social and economic scale came Martin, Azo, Ulf and another Lambert. They paid only a penny a year.

This survey of Pytchley emphasizes the complex web of feudal relationships that defined rural life in the early Middle Ages. As in Pytchley, so in the rest of the country: villeins were the most numerous class in a population that grew from around 1.5 million in the late eleventh century to a peak of somewhere between five million and six million in 1300, before plummeting to about three million after the great plague outbreaks of the mid-fourteenth century. They owned nothing of their own, in law at least. All they had belonged to their lord, and he was entitled to a whole series of dues and fines from them. Not only did they have to work his land for an agreed period as well as their own holdings, but when their daughters married, the villeins had to pay merchet, a fine to the lord. They had to pay wood-silver for the right to gather wood in their lord's forests. They had to pay arbitrary taxes to their lord. They had to pay to have their corn ground by the lord's miller, their bread baked by the lord's baker. They could even be sold or granted to another lord. And when they died, the heir had to hand over a heriot, generally the best beast on the holding.

However, in practice this rather bleak picture of a life of virtual slavery, with labour and money being extracted from poor villagers at every turn, was often less harsh than it

ILLUSTRATION FROM JOHN FITZHERBERT, *NEW TRACTE FOR HUSBAND MEN, c. 1525.*

seems. A villein did not have to work his lord's land personally, for example, he could send one of his sons, and if he had any sense he would provide the son who was least use to him at home. On most manors, the working day finished at three o'clock in the afternoon or earlier. And in spite of the apparent rigidity of the social hierarchy, it was by no means always clear who actually *was* a bondsman. Various legal disputes over the ownership of land in the twelfth and thirteenth centuries involved a great deal of wrangling over whether one party was or was not a villein, suggesting that the status of individuals within the feudal system was less straightforward than it might appear.

WORKING THE LORD'S LAND WAS REQUIRED OF MEDIEVAL VILLEINS; HUNTING THERE, HOWEVER, WAS PROHIBITED.

Intriguing though it is, this vignette of medieval life in Pytchley poses as many questions as it answers. It tells us nothing, for example, of the wives, sons and daughters who also lived and worked in the village. It says little of the stock held by the villagers, beyond the fact that they had plough-teams – an eight-ox team was the norm – and poultry to provide the eggs. (The demesne farm boasted thirty oxen in four teams, 220 sheep, twenty pigs and 'ten old sheep in their second year'.) Neither does it tell us anything of the general layout of the village itself, or of the homes the villagers lived in.

It is rather dangerous to speculate over the size, shape, even the very existence of an early medieval village. Domesday, usually held to provide evidence of the presence of early vil-

lages, is in fact a record of land holdings rather than settlements, and there are many cases of villages once thought to have been referred to in that survey which have been shown by archaeological excavation to date from a century or so after 1086. Christopher Taylor cites the case of Faxton in Northamptonshire, long thought on the evidence of Domesday to have been a village with a population of sixty to eighty people in the late eleventh century. The site is now deserted. Large-scale excavation found a clear pattern of medieval cottages laid out in rows lining the main streets of the village, but nothing dated from any earlier than 1150. As Taylor says, 'It appears therefore that the medieval village of Faxton did not exist in 1086 and that the place called Faxton, apparently described in the Domesday Book, must have lain elsewhere or was not a village at all.' The truth may be that Faxton, like many of the 'villages' mentioned in Domesday, was no more than a widely dispersed arrangement of farmsteads and smaller houses spread over the manor.

By the thirteenth century, however, nucleated villages had appeared all over the countryside, often as a result of the growth, movement or amalgamation of tiny hamlets and individual farmsteads. Agriculture was usually practised through the open-field system: two or (more rarely) three or four common fields were divided into strips, and the holdings of individual tenants were inter-mixed with those of their neighbours. Strips were grouped together in furlongs. The lord's own holdings were also in these fields, although they were often consolidated into furlongs, and the arrangement was far from static. Land might be reallotted among the villagers on a more or less regular basis. One tenant might take over some or all of his neighbour's holding for one reason or another, or perhaps the lord himself would initiate change. A twelfth-century lord of the manor of Great Sturton in Lincolnshire, in granting some of his demesne lands to Kirkstead Abbey, recorded that

since the furlongs of my demesne lie mixed among the lands of my men and the monks wish to dwell apart from others I have therefore brought together the land of my demesne and the land of my men in the further part of the fields and I have given that land to the monks to have together, and I have given to my men for their part of the

AN ESTATE MAP BY T.LANGDON,1606, SHOWS FIELDS DIVIDED INTO STRIPS OF INDIVIDUAL HOLDINGS.

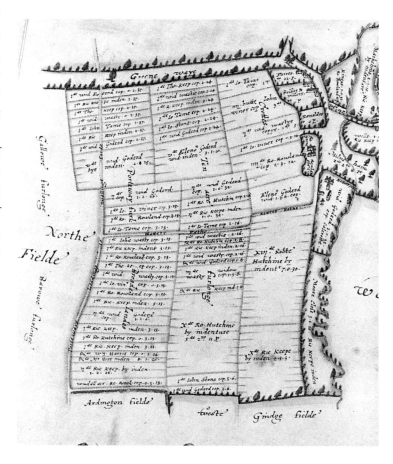

land which they had, an exchange from the land of my demesne at their pleasure.

Medieval agriculture is a vast and often highly contentious subject among present-day scholars. How, when and to what extent crop rotation was practised; the ins and outs of the infield-outfield system (the 'infield' closest to the village was cultivated every year while the 'outfield' was divided in two, with one part lying fallow for a few years and then being cultivated, and the other part left largely uncultivated); the fact that in some areas of the country such as Kent, individual strips could be divided among sons, or that in others where pastoral farming predominated, like the West Country, fields were enclosed rather than open – these are fascinating topics. But barring a detailed discussion of the complexities of different agrarian systems, what is of interest here is that the straightforward open-field system, to take the commonest example, required a high degree of organization. Few villeins had enough oxen for a complete plough-team, so they had to pool resources. Ditches and drains that ran beside each strip had to be kept clear, or one's neighbour's land would be flooded as well as one's own. Besides grazing the meadows, stock was allowed onto the strips between harvest and sowing, so both procedures had to be coordinated and carried out in common.

For these operations to work successfully, everybody had to pull together, and as a result the medieval village was inevitably a very tightknit community. Village assemblies were regularly held to decide on planning and timetables, and rules were set down. Surviving regulations for the care of the common fields at Wymeswold in Leicestershire in the early fifteenth century, for example, show a high degree of codification. Among other things they provide that certain areas be thrown open to grazing 'on Crow-chemesseday', 14 September, and that anyone who breaks with this shall pay a penny to the church for each beast; that 'men or women that have no peas of their own growing, let them gather them twice in the week of Wednesday and on Friday, reasonably going in the land furrows and gathering with their hands and with no sickles, once before noon and no more'; that no man or woman glean the corn 'that is able to work for his meat and twopence a day at the least to help to save his neighbour's corn'.

Manorial courts could also enforce certain behaviours. Surviving records are full of fines for various offences against the public (and occasionally private) good:

Peter Clark of Shepreth encroached on the furlong of Metlemadwe to a width of four feet, and hath not made amends despite many previous orders.

John Kersey fined 12d for diverting the brook which flows through the middle of the manor, to a width of half a foot, and causing a nuisance.

*William Cock lodged foreigners at harvest-time to the detriment of the
whole village, fined 6d.*

*Richard Legat fornicated with Mathilda Heyke, a kinswoman, whereby the
manor land suffered serious harm; fined 40d.*

One can only wonder at the harm done to the manor land referred to in the last example.
However, the mention of 'foreigners' (i.e., people from outside the area) in the previous
entry reinforces the importance of the medieval village as essentially an inward-looking
community. Those who do not belong are regularly referred to as 'foreigners' or 'strangers'.
And in spite of the fact that the manor was the most significant administrative unit in theory, in practice it was the village that mattered to its inhabitants. The two were far from
being synonymous – some manors comprised a number of villages, while other villages
spread across the boundaries of two or even three manors.

Imagine that you have to build yourself a house. You have no specialist skills and no

OCCUPATIONS OF THE RURAL PEASANTS, 1502.

money to buy them in, no plans, no measuring instruments, no help apart from friends and family. The only tools at your disposal are basic cutting and shaping implements – axes, adzes, chisels and the like – and the only materials you can use are those that you can find or forage in the immediate neighbourhood.

This, broadly speaking, was the position of the medieval peasant. And given those limitations, it is scarcely surprisingly that his or her cottage was often a fairly primitive affair, or that it fell to pieces within a couple of generations. Excavations of medieval dwellings at Wharram Percy in North Yorkshire, for example, show that complete rebuilding took place every thirty years or so. And complete it must have been, over and above any running repairs that were carried out, since for some reason each new cottage was usually given a slightly different alignment from the house that it replaced.

In the years following the Conquest, and probably for three or four centuries after that, most peasants' cottages were either mud huts or primitive wood-framed structures, rather than the attractive stone or half-timbered houses that one often thinks of as medieval. Small though these latter examples are by contemporary standards, they are usually either much later, or much higher up the social scale. The homes of cottagers and the lower ranks of villeins were *really* small. A cottage that was excavated at Seacourt in Berkshire was only ten by twelve feet, while another at Wharram Percy measured ten by twenty.

Although no examples of peasant homes survive from the Middle Ages, we can piece together some idea of them from archaeological and documentary evidence and from later practice. Maurice Barley, in *The English Farmhouse and Cottage*, cites the example of barkpeelers in Cumberland who in the early twentieth century were still building themselves temporary shelters. They used pairs of poles lashed together at the top and joined by a horizontal ridge pole, and built walls of earth two feet high that were kept intact by skins of wattle, and a roof of turf. These huts were thirteen by eight feet, and they probably came as close as anything to the medieval cottage, except that they were provided with stone-built hearths and chimneys – a luxury that no medieval peasant enjoyed.

The majority of cottages in the early Middle Ages were of one storey and rectangular in plan, containing only a single room which functioned as living area, sleeping accommodation and kitchen. The choice of building materials depended on availability and economy. Stone was out – it was too expensive, too difficult to transport and too hard to work. Mud, mixed with straw and gravel, was probably much more common and, like cob, it continued to be used in parts of the southwest right up into the nineteenth century. Cheap, easy to work and easy to obtain, so long as the local soil had enough lime to enable it to set, it was applied in layers about six inches high and three feet wide. Each layer was trodden down and allowed to dry before the next was applied. We do not know if the walls of medieval mud cottages were given any protective coatings, like their later counterparts. Most likely they

A LATE-MEDIEVAL NATIVITY SCENE SHOWING CRUDE TIMBER-FRAME CONSTRUCTION TYPICAL OF THE PERIOD.

ALTHOUGH HUNTING WAS AN IMPORTANT PART OF THE PEASANT ECONOMY, IT WAS STRICTLY

REGULATED, AND FINES WERE IMPOSED EVEN FOR THE KEEPING OF HUNTING DOGS.

First in a morning when thou art waked, and purposest to rise, lift up thy hands, and bless thee, and make a sign of the holy cross, *In nomine patris, et filii, et spiritus sancti*. Amen. In the name of the father, the son, and the holy ghost. And if thou say a Pater noster, an Ave, and a Creed, and remember thy maker, thou shalt speed much the better. And when thou art up and ready, then first sweep thy house, dress up thy dishboard, and set all things in good order within thy house: milk thy kine, suckle thy calves, see up thy milk, take up thy children and array them, and provide for thy husband's breakfast, dinner, supper, and for thy children and servants, and take thy part with them.

And to ordain corn and malt to the mill, to bake and brew withall when need is. And meet it to the mill,

and from the mill, and see that thou have thy measure again beside the toll, or else the miller dealeth not truly with thee, or else thy corn is not dry as it should be.

Thou must make butter and cheese when thou may, serve thy swine both morning and evening, and give thy poultry meat in the morning; and when time of the year cometh, thou must take heed how the hens, ducks, and geese do lay, and to gather up their eggs, and when they wax broody, to set them there as no beasts, swine, nor other vermin hurt them. And thou must know that all whole-footed fowls will sit a month, and all cloven-footed fowls will sit but three weeks, except a peahen, and great fowls, as cranes, bustards, and such other. And when they have brought forth their birds, to see that they be well kept . . .

And in the beginning of March, or a little afore, is the time for a wife to make her garden, and to get as many good seeds and herbs as she can, and especially such as be good for the pot, and to eat. And as oft as need shall require, it must be weeded, for else the weeds will overgrow the herbs.

And also in March is time to sow flax and hemp . . . but how it should be sown, weeded, pulled, rippled, watered, washed, dried, beaten, breaked, tawed, heckled, spun, wound, wrapped, and woven, it needeth not for me to show, for there be ways enough. And thereof may they make sheets, boardcloths, towels, shirts, smocks, and such other necessaries, and therefore let thy distaff be always ready for a pastime, that thou be not idle.

And undoubted a woman cannot get her living honestly with spinning on the distaff, but it stoppeth a gap, and must needs be had. The bolls of flax, when they be rippled off, must be riddled from the weeds, and made dry with the sun, to get out the seeds. How be it one manner of linseed . . . will not open by the sun: and therefore, when they be dry, they must be sore bruised and broken, the wives know how, and then winnowed and kept dry, till their time come again. Thy female hemp must be pulled from the churl hemp, for that beareth no seed, and thou must do by it, as thou didst by the flax. The churl hemp beareth seed, and beware the birds eat it not, as it groweth: the hemp thereof is on so good as the female hemp, but yet it will do good service . . .

It is convenient for a husband to have sheep of his own, for many causes, and then may his wife have part of the wool to make her husband and herself some clothes. And at the least way, she may have the locks of the sheep, either to make clothes or blankets and coverlets, or both. And if she have no wool of her own, she may take wool to spin of cloth-makers, and by that means she may have a convenient living, and many times to do other works. It is a wife's occupation, to winnow all manner of corns, to make malt, to wash and wring, to make hay, shear corn, and in time of need to help her husband to fill the muck-wain or dung-cart, drive the plough, to load hay, corn, and such other. And to go or ride to the market, to sell butter, cheese, milk, eggs, chickens, capons, hens, pigs, geese, and all manner of corns. And also to buy all manner of necessary things belonging to households, and to make a true reckoning and account to her husband, what she hath paid. And if the husband go to the market, to buy or sell, as they often do, he then to show his wife in like manner. For if one of them should use to deceive the other, he deceiveth himself, and he is not like to thrive. And therefore they must be true either to other.

I could peradventure show the husbands diverse points that the wives deceive them in and in like manner, how husbands deceive their wives: but if I should do so, I should show no subtle points of deception than either of them knew before.

From *The Book of Husbandry of Master Fitzherbert*, 1534

were, since mud walling is extremely susceptible to weathering. Thatch was the almost universal roofing material and, if well maintained, would keep the rain from seeping downwards and causing the walls to crumble. But the most primitive cottages probably did not stand on any sort of plinth, other than beaten earth, and rising damp would have ensured that within a decade or two the walls would begin to collapse.

The most common of all medieval building materials was wood, and across virtually the whole of England, with the exception of the extreme southwest and parts of East Anglia, timber was the usual choice for a cottage, and cruck construction the usual method of employing it. No one is sure where cruck building originated. In Victorian times it was thought to have developed from boat-building and/or to have been brought from Scandinavia by the Vikings. More recent evidence from archaeological studies of several early buildings in Ireland suggest different, perhaps Celtic, roots. Wherever it came from, the method was wonderfully simple. The word 'cruck' is a variant of the Middle English 'crook' in the sense of a hook or curve, and derives from the fact that the main load-bearing timbers, the blades, were often curved – although both straight and jointed crucks are also known. Two blades – often halves of the same piece of timber to ensure some symmetry – were positioned to form a triangle open at its base, and pegged together just below their apex, so that a 'V' was left above the point where they crossed. A second cruck truss was put together in the same way. They were connected at their apexes by a ridge-beam and some way down their sides by a pair of horizontal timbers or purlins. The space between the two pairs of blades was called a bay.

The whole assembly was reared upright using ropes, and the feet of the blades were rammed a foot or so into holes in the ground, having been scorched to prevent them from rotting. The frame thus created was rather like a large ridge tent, all roof and no walls, perhaps fifteen feet high and anywhere between nine and sixteen feet long. In its most primitive form the structure would be clad with thatch or turf over a lattice of branches and twigs. An opening for a doorway was left in one of the trusses, and there was just one room inside, open to the roof.

Neither permanence nor stability was a feature of early cruck houses. The Irish saga of *The Feast of Bricru* talks of how a house was inadvertently pushed over and had to be given a good shove to get it upright again, and there are instances throughout the Middle Ages of individual cottages, and even whole villages, being blown away in strong winds. But there were various improvements to the basic theme, many of which both increased the strength of the frame and provided more space inside the house. From at least the mid-thirteenth century, it became common for the feet of the

MOST EARLY MEDIEVAL COTTAGES WERE BUILT USING CRUCK CONSTRUCTION. THE UPPER FLOOR WAS USED AS A SLEEPING LOFT, OR STOREROOM OR BOTH.

blades to be set into a sill-beam resting on a stone plinth, more effective in preventing rising damp than just scorching them and setting them directly into the ground. But then a tie-beam was needed to counteract the outward thrust. Halved into the blades about a third or half of the way up to form a giant 'A' shape, tie-beams improved stability and offered the chance to insert another chamber in the upper part of the cottage. Reached by a ladder, the upstairs room would have been cramped, certainly, but at least more efficient use was made of the available space. It is hard to say exactly what this use was, however. Today, we are accustomed to thinking of a house, however small, having separate areas for living and sleeping. The medieval cottager made no such distinction, and while the upper floor of his cottage may have been some sort of sleeping loft, it also might have functioned as a storeroom.

WATTLE-WORK WAS PLASTERED OVER WITH A MIXTURE OF MUD, STRAW, COW HAIR AND COW DUNG.

If tie-beams were made to extend out beyond the line of the blades, then as well as supporting an upper storey, they could carry longitudinal horizontal beams, wall-plates, which helped to support the roof. From here it was only a short step to the introduction of vertical walls fixed between wall-plate and sill-beam. Studwork frames were infilled with wattle and daub – wooden hurdles or wattle-work plastered with a mixture of mud, chopped straw, cow hair and cow dung. The walls provided a little more space inside the cottage, and allowed a doorway to be set in the side rather than in the end wall. There was no real contribution to the structural integrity of the building, since these walls were not load-bearing in any way, but this meant that the infill could easily be replaced at a later date by brick or stone, as often happened in many of the grander examples that survive.

Cruck construction meant that it was relatively easy to build a house of more than one bay. Three, four or five pairs of blades could be linked together – as many as you liked or could afford. At Leigh Court, a mile south of Worcester, there is a huge cruck barn over 150 feet long, which dates from around the beginning of the fourteenth century. It has no fewer than eleven trusses. But Leigh Court Barn is exceptional. For a house, two, three or four bays were common, and no medieval cottage would have consisted of more than one or two. Internal trusses usually omitted the tie-beam, having only a collar-beam pegged and jointed into the blades much closer to the apex. Occasionally all trusses had blades that only reached up to a collar-beam, a method known as 'base-cruck' construction.

Large numbers of cruck buildings still survive in a great swathe from Hampshire up to Northumberland and across from the north and east of Wales to the east midlands. Leicestershire has around forty, Herefordshire some 130. The magnificent Cotswold stone roof of the mid-thirteenth-century Great Coxwell Barn near Faringdon is supported by a system of alternating aisle-posts and base-crucks. Two small cruck-built houses in Berkshire have recently been dated to the thirteenth century. There is a good group at Harwell in Oxfordshire, two at least of which date from the early fifteenth century. And in the north of England cruck construction continued right up into the early nineteenth centuries.

Cruck-frames are hardly ever found in the extreme west, perhaps because of a short age of suitable timber. Nor do they survive in Lincolnshire, East Anglia or the southeast; this may imply that the form disappeared much earlier in these areas than in the rest of the country, perhaps as a result of influences from the European mainland. The architectural historian Basil Oliver, after describing a beautiful cruck house at Sutton Bonington, Nottinghamshire, as 'efficient, but ugly' (*The Cottages of England*, 1929), offered the explanation that 'the more architecturally sensitive natives of the south-eastern group of counties would never have tolerated so unsightly a form of construction'.

The vast majority of surviving timber-framed buildings employ one of two other construction techniques – box-framing and post-and-truss. In contrast to the cruck house, where sloping timbers carry the load down to the ground, the box-frame involves the use of heavy upright posts that bear the weight of the roof. These are placed at reasonably regular intervals along the whole length of a side wall – in fact, to all intents and purposes they *are* the wall – and because they provide a continuous bearing, there is no need to divide the building into bays. Post-and-truss construction has more in common with the cruck, but instead of two or more 'A'-shaped trusses carrying the weight, two upright posts are joined together at the top by a horizontal tie-beam. The principal rafters are fitted onto this beam and held together by a collar-beam, which is braced by two vertical timbers jointed into

THE DETAIL SHOWS TIMBER-FRAMING IN-FILLED WITH FLINT.

A TIMBER-FRAMED COTTAGE AT LEINTHALL IN STAFFORDSHIRE.

the tie-beam at the bottom and the collar-beam at the top. As with the cruck house, the walls between the posts make no contribution to the structural integrity of the building, although various arrangements of diagonal struts and braces were often introduced.

Thousands of examples of timber-framed buildings survive around the country, from the spectacular Guildhall at Lavenham in Suffolk to the picture-postcard delights of Little Moreton Hall in Cheshire. There are small houses, like the fourteenth-century Clergy House at Alfriston in Sussex, and huge mansions, like the Tudor Speke Hall, Liverpool. There are Wealden houses, with their upper storeys jettied out, and Kentish yeoman houses with their centres recessed in.

But, in spite of the fact that every second timber-framed house in England is today described as a cottage, there is nothing that a medieval peasant would have recognized as home. Most smaller houses date from the sixteenth and seventeenth centuries or, if they do have medieval origins, they were built as substantial farmhouses or yeoman farmsteads. The typical farmhouse was of three or four bays, with doorways in each of its long sides, facing each other and linked by a cross passage. This passage opened directly into a two-bay hall. If the house was grand enough, there might be a screen of sorts dividing off the cross-passage from the hall to keep out the draughts, as was common in the homes of the landed classes. One can still see the arrangement in practice at many castles and country houses. Haddon Hall in Derbyshire is a good example where a fixed screen of *c.*1450 forms a partition between the main entrance way and the Great Hall. Beyond the screen there are doorways to the service areas of the house, the kitchen, buttery and pantry.

The farmer's home perhaps had a kitchen, dairy and brewhouse leading off to one side of the cross passage. In some houses, though, this part of the building was reserved for

ALFRISTON CLERGY
HOUSE IN EAST SUSSEX,
14TH CENTURY.

A KENTISH FARMHOUSE. TILE-HANGING WAS INTRODUCED IN THE 16TH
CENTURY AND WAS GENERALLY CONFINED TO THE SOUTHEAST.

animals. Although contemporary references to people and stock living together under the same roof are rare, Trevor Rowley notes the case of William de Hampton of Hallow in Worcestershire, who, in 1340, made over his house and holdings to his daughter and son-in-law. They were to pay an annual rent of six shillings, and William reserved the right to keep his oxen in stalls in their house.

The hall was the main living and cooking area. It would be open to the rafters, with a fire in the centre. There was no chimney – the smoke was allowed to escape (or not, as the case may be) through a louvre in the roof or 'wind-eyes' in the walls. Later in the Middle Ages the practice developed of jettying an upper floor out into the hall, leaving only one bay (the 'smoke-bay') open. Windows were small and unglazed, with wooden bars and shutters, and the floor was clay, perhaps mixed with oxblood and ashes to create a hard surface. There may have been a second room beyond the hall, a *bower*. The word is Anglo-Saxon and denoted any room that wasn't a hall, rather like 'chamber', which gradually replaced it during the Middle Ages.

Furniture was scant. A table, usually just a board resting on a trestle frame, was the most important piece in the hall, and the family sat on benches or stools. Their food was prepared over the open fire in the kitchen, if there was one, or more often in the hall itself. Pottage, a sort of semi-liquid stew, was the staple hot food. 'Potage is not so much used in all Christendom as it is used in England,' wrote Andrew Boorde in 1542, '[it] is made of the liquor in the which flesh is sodden in, with putting-to chopped herbs, and oatmeal and salt.' As a result, one of the commonest pieces of cooking equipment in the ordinary medieval home was the cauldron, which stood on a tripod over the fire.

CENTRAL OPEN FIRES BECAME RARER AS THE 16TH CENTURY PROGRESSED.

An early medieval source quoted by Sara Paston-Williams (*The Art of Dining*, 1993) sets out the basic requirements for a kitchen in a great house:

There should be a small table on which cabbage may be minced and also lentils, peas, shelled beans, beans in the pod, millet, onions, and other vegetables of the kind that can be cut up. There should also be pots, tripods, a mortar, a hatchet, a pestle, a stirring stick, a hook, a cauldron, a bronze vessel, small pitchers, a trencher, a bowl, a platter, a pickling vat and knives for cleaning fish . . . The chief cook should have a cupboard in the kitchen where he may store many aromatic spices, and bread flour sifted through a sieve may be hidden there . . . Likewise there should be a large spoon for removing foam and skimming.

Households lower down the social scale would have more or less of this equipment. Roger the Dyer, for example, a wealthy craftsman who lived in a four-roomed house in Colchester in 1301, had in his kitchen one brass pot worth 20d. and a tripod worth 4d., as well as a brass posnet, which was a sort of all-in-one pot and tripod with a handle. Presumably he also owned various smaller items that the tax assessors who inventoried his property didn't think it worthwhile mentioning. Even his much poorer neighbour, Alice Reyner (who only possessed '1 poor robe worth 2s.', in contrast to his '2 garments 20s.') owned a brass posnet. Vessels of wood, leather and earthenware were also common.

'POTAGE IS NOT SO MUCH USED IN ALL CHRISTENDOM AS IT IS USED IN ENGLAND.' – ANDREW BOORDE, 1542.

Roger the Dyer also owned two beds, but Alice's tax assessment doesn't mention one. The homes of the rich contained quite elaborate beds – in *The Booke of the Duchesse* (1369) Chaucer describes a feather bed 'Of down of pure dowve's white . . . Rayed with gold, and ryght wel cled/In fyn blak satyn' from beyond the sea. The middling sort of merchant and tradesman, and even prosperous villeins, might have freestanding wooden beds, but cottagers had to make do with straw pallets or rough mats that were dragged out for use each night.

Two of the most vivid accounts of life in the medieval cottage come from literature. The widow in Chaucer's *Nun's Priest's Tale* lived in a 'narwe cotage/Biside a grove, stondynge in a dale'. It consisted of two rooms – a hall and a bower – and both were blackened by the smoke from the open fire: 'Ful sooty was hire bour and eek hir halle'. Outside, there was a yard 'enclosed al aboute with stikkes, and a drye dych withoute'.

What was day-to-day life like for this 'povre wydwe' and the two daughters who lived with her? She didn't own a great deal, the poet tells us, but her possessions nevertheless included three sows, three cattle, a sheep called Malle and, of course, Chauntecleer and Pertelote, the cock and hen that are the main characters in the *Nun's Priest's Tale*. The three women lived a simple life. They ate no dainty morsels or sauces, drank no wine, and subsisted largely on milk, brown bread, a little broiled bacon and an egg or two.

William Langland's *Vision of Piers Plowman*, probably written in the 1360s, presents a much starker image of cottage life. Langland makes a plea for

the poor in the cottage,
Charged with a crew of children and with a landlord's rent.
What they win by their spinning to make their porridge with,
Milk and meal, to satisfy the babes,
The babes that continually cry for food –
This they must spend on the rent of their houses;
And themselves suffer with hunger,
With woe in winter, rising a-nights
In the narrow room to rock the cradle.
Pitiful is it to read the cottage women's woe,
Aye, and many another that puts a good face on it,
Ashamed to beg, ashamed to let neighbours know
All that they need, noontide and evening.
Many the children, and nought but a man's hands
To clothe and feed them; and few pennies come in,
And many mouths to eat the pennies up.
Bread and thin ale for them are a banquet . . .

Two points are worth making about Langland's vision of the poor cottager. One is that it makes clear village life in the Middle Ages was not the subsistence economy we often suppose it to have been. Although the peasants kept animals (even poor Alice Reyner in Colchester had a pig valued at two shillings), worked their own land and bartered with their neighbours for goods and services, hard cash was still needed for clothes, tools, cooking equipment and the like.

The other point is that in spite of Langland's heartrending description of 'the babes that continually cry for food', most peasant households were actually quite small, consisting of no more than four or five people. There are several reasons for this. Evidence from the Tudor period suggests that the poor tended to delay marriage until they were in their mid-twenties, probably because of the need to save enough money to set up house on their own or to wait for the death of a father. The support network of the extended family of parents, children, children's spouses and grandchildren all living under the same roof, was rare in England. Late marriage effectively cut short a woman's childbearing years (she was likely to reach the menopause at around the age of forty). Fertility was also reduced by malnutrition and by the length of time a woman breastfed, commonly eighteen months or more. In addition both fertility and family size were reduced by premature death. A marriage that lasted much more than twenty years was the exception rather than the rule, and high rates of stillbirths, miscarriages and infant mortality make the picture of the medieval peasant and his wife crowded together in their

ILLUSTRATION FROM *FABLES OF ESOPE*, 1484. THE MOST VIVID ACCOUNTS OF LIFE IN THE MEDIEVAL COTTAGE COME FROM LITERATURE.

one- or two-room cottage with a sprawling horde of babies, toddlers and adolescents quite a rarity.

Chaucer's widow and Langland's poor cottagers lived in a world that had changed quite dramatically from the one that the villeins and cottars of Pytchley had known in the early twelfth century. England had been, was still being, decimated by the plague outbreaks of 1348-9, 1361-2, 1369 and 1375, which contributed to a fall in the population of somewhere between one-third and forty per cent. The chronicler Henry Knighton left a vivid account of the spread of the disease:

> *This dreadful pestilence penetrated through the coastal regions and came from Southampton to Bristol, and almost the whole strength of the town perished, as if overcome by sudden death, for few there were who kept their beds more than two or three days . . . at Leicester in the little parish of St Leonard's more than 380 people perished, in the parish of the Holy Cross 400, in the parish of St Margaret 700 . . . the cruel death spread everywhere, following the course of the sun.*

Some villages were devastated to such an extent that they never recovered and were eventually abandoned. Others escaped untouched. But the long-term implications for the cottager were even more far-reaching.

Initially, the survivors benefited from the widespread labour shortages. There were hasty attempts to maintain both wage levels and social structures. 'No man shall pay or promise to pay to any man more wages, liveries, hire or salaries than is accustomed', said an Ordinance of 1349. Feudal obligations were to be strictly enforced, and those bondsmen who refused to serve were to be imprisoned. But wages crept up steadily, and landlords, finding it more and more difficult to replace tenants, were compelled to reduce rents and offer attractive terms. If they did not, their land would lie uncultivated. Maurice Keen cites the example of the Beaumont estates in Leicestershire, where in 1427 the manor of Whitwick had twelve out of thirty-one houses lying empty, and 289 acres of land gone to waste. At Markfield nearly half the houses were in decay, and at Hugglescote ten holdings had been taken in hand by the lord because there were no tenants to farm them. The system by which villeins were bonded to their lord, and owed him all the customary dues referred to earlier, had not been abolished, but it was simply impracticable for a lord to enforce it, and during the fifteenth century it all but disappeared. Dues were commuted to cash rents, and villeins gave way to tenants who paid fixed sums for a lease that lasted for perhaps three lives, without being liable to the arbitrary taxation which had been a feature of the manorial system. Moreover, they could sell that lease on to another without the lord intervening, providing they paid an entry fine to have the change registered.

The other major change to take place in the English rural scene after the Black Death followed on from this. Pastoral farming, and the enclosing of lands to facilitate it, became more attractive to a great landowner. He needed fewer men to maintain a flock of sheep or a herd of cattle than he did for arable cultivation, and the profits could be good. But enclosure meant eviction for many cottagers, it meant the demolition of their homes, it might even mean the destruction of whole settlements. An early-sixteenth-century document described this change in practice on the Prior of Bicester's estates:

'. . . THOSE MESSUAGES WERE LAID WASTE AND THROWN DOWN, AND LANDS FORMERLY USED FOR ARABLE HE TURNED OVER TO PASTURE FOR ANIMALS.'

> *He held this land on the second of March 1489 when those messuages were laid waste and thrown down, and lands formerly used for arable he turned over to pasture for animals, so three ploughs are now out of use there, and eighteen people who used to work on that land and earn their living there and who dwelled in the houses have gone away to take to the roads in their misery, and to seek their bread elsewhere and so are led into idleness.*

The same year that the Prior was wreaking such havoc on a rural community (it was Wretchwick in Oxfordshire), the Crown was taking steps to halt the process. 'Great inconvenience daily doth increase by desolation and pulling down and wilfull waste of houses and Towns . . . and laying to pasture lands which customarily have been used in tillage', said the preamble to an Act which made it illegal to convert open fields to pasturage, if this involved destroying holdings of more than twenty acres. 'Idleness – ground and beginning of all mischiefs – daily doth increase, for where in some Towns two hundred persons were occupied and lived by their lawful labours, now be there occupied 2 or 3 herdmen and the residue fallen in idleness.'

Not every cottager in the land was so affected, of course. Employers might not like having to pay higher wages, but many stuck to arable farming and stumped up the extra, to the benefit of the rural labourers who made up the bulk of the cottage-dwelling population. Indeed, some prospered, perhaps even renting larger holdings to farm themselves, and perhaps enlisting the services of the village carpenter to replace their one- or two-room house with something rather sturdier.

CHAPTER II

The Great
Rebuilding
1550-1690

Of one bay's breadth, God wot! a silly cote,
Whose thatched sparres are furr'd with sluttish soote
A whole inch thick, shining like black-moor's brows,
Through smok that down the head-les barrel blows:
At his bed's-feete feeden his stalled teme;
His swine beneath, his pullen ore the beame:
A starved tenement.

JOSEPH HALL, *SATIRES*, c.1610

By the later sixteenth century the architecture of the English countryside was more diverse and exciting than it had ever been. The great rambling courtyard houses that had served as local power bases of medieval warlords were being overshadowed by the buildings put up for a new breed of Tudor courtier, ambitious and entrepreneurial landowners who had benefited from the massive sell-off of monastic estates in the wake of the Dissolution. Taking just three examples from one county, Wiltshire, there was William Sharington, who converted the Augustinian abbey at Lacock in Wiltshire into a house in the 1540s before being imprisoned in 1549 for diverting the produce of the Bristol Mint, of which he was vice-treasurer, into his own pocket. William Herbert, first Earl of Pembroke, was granted the nunnery estate of Wilton in 1544 (according to Aubrey, Herbert went down on his knees to beg forgiveness from the Abbess when the nuns returned with the accession of Mary I, only to appear on the doorstep the minute the Queen died, crying 'Out, ye Whores, to worke, to worke, ye Whores, goe spinne'). And John Thynne bought the Carthusian priory at Longleat for £53 in 1541, and over the next forty years transformed it into one of the greatest of all Elizabethan houses at a cost that greatly exceeded his original outlay – £8,016.13s.8d.

'When men sought to cure mortality by fame . . . buildings were the only way', wrote Francis Bacon, and his contemporaries proved him right. Elizabeth's chief minister, William Cecil, spent most of the reign building Burghley, near Stamford, and Theobalds in Hertfordshire. Christopher Hatton, soon to be the Queen's Lord Chancellor, built Holdenby, Northamptonshire, in the 1570s – a house described by Cecil in 1579 as having 'a great magnificence in the front or front pieces of the house, and so every part answerable to [the] other, to allure liking'. In the 1580s and 1590s the architect Robert Smythson was creating a spectacular group of country houses in the Midlands, including the flamboyant Wollaton Hall in Nottinghamshire (1580-88, for Sir Francis Willoughby) and Hardwick Hall, Derbyshire (1590-97, for Elizabeth, Countess of Shrewsbury, 'Bess of Hardwick').

The idea that architecture was an effective way of displaying one's status and wealth had come to stay, and it reached down from the great landowners of the sixteenth century to the merchants and farmers who, in spite of periodic crises, were generally doing rather well out of the expanding Tudor economy. When Thomas Paycocke married

Margaret Harrold at Coggeshall in Essex in the early 1500s, his father John, a wealthy clothier, marked the occasion by erecting a timber-framed building of five bays that combined living accommodation with business premises. The studding is so close that the infill panels are scarcely wider than timbers themselves – a decorative rather than a structural feature. A carved bressumer stretches across the whole of the front of the building and is ornamented with an array of curious devices – a dragon, a figure diving into a lily, a head perched on a stalk, a king and queen entwined together. Inside, the hall ceiling is brilliantly carved with tracery and the Paycockes' merchant mark of an ermine tail. As well as being a workplace – the roof space was used to store wool before it went out to local cloth-makers, and the ground at the back functioned as a tentering yard, where lengths of cloth were stretched out to dry after fulling – Paycocke's was every bit as much a statement of its owner's wealth and social position as Burghley or Wollaton.

For those with money, land and enterprise, Tudor England was the right place and the right time. Prices rose dramatically during the sixteenth century, notwithstanding various troughs and peaks, and by 1600 they stood at around 550% of what they had been a century earlier. Standards of living in the countryside rose too, not only for the Protestant courtiers who were the main beneficiaries of royal patronage, or the merchants and lawyers who did so well out of an expanding economy and an increasingly litigious society, but for the middling sort, the farmers and village craftsmen. These, perhaps, rather than the ordinary cottage labourer, were the people referred to by Lupold von Wedel, a Pomeranian soldier of fortune who toured England in 1585:

> *I have seen peasants presenting themselves statelier in manner, and keeping a more sumptuous table than some noblemen do in Germany. That is a poor peasant who has no silver-gilt salt-cellars, silver cups, and spoons.*

The word 'peasant' encompassed a wide range of social groupings in the sixteenth century, especially to an outsider who was unacquainted with the country. Philip Julius, the Duke of Stettin-Pomerania, also toured the country, this time in 1602. His secretary, Jacob Gerschow, noted with surprise that after coursing a hare for a day an Englishman would often leave it to his dogs, because 'the game is less thought of than the amusement. This is the case even with the peasants, who also are permitted to hunt; they keep fine big dogs, at little expense, for with a little money they can procure the heads, entrails, and feet of lambs and calves, which in England are always thrown away, with the exception of the tongue.' This may have been true of the yeoman farmer, but the idea of the labourer keeping 'fine big dogs' and buying offal to feed them is a little hard to take. The ordinary cottager, whose wages had perhaps doubled as against the five- or six-fold increase in prices, was having a hard time of it.

Yet it seemed in the last years of the Tudors that everyone was building – courtiers,

merchants, even farmers and labourers. In his 1577 *Description of England* William Harrison, the rector of Radwinter in Essex, reckoned that 'every man almost is a builder, and he that hath bought any small parcel of ground, be it never so little, will not be quiet till he have pulled down the old house (if any were there standing) and set up a new after his own device'. Perhaps the main reason behind this building boom, over and above the emergence of architecture as an important indicator of social status, was that there were more people in need of houses. In fact there were more people, full stop. After the depredations of the plague in the fourteenth century, the population was rising again and, since the custom of a newly married couple living under the same roof with parents or parents-in-law was as rare in Tudor England as it had been in the Middle Ages, more houses were required. Some forty new families appeared in the little village of Foxton in Cambridgeshire in the second half of the sixteenth century, and between 1550 and 1620 more than fifty new houses were built there – some replacing older buildings, but others put up on spare ground. At Epworth in Lincolnshire, one hundred new cottages were built between 1580 and 1630. Numbers of cottages were put up in Oxfordshire, most of them single-bay and only ten by twelve feet, and in Rockingham Forest, the pressure on the existing housing stock was such that farmbuildings, stables and barns were converted for residential use. A timber-framed

HOME AND THE HOMELESS. A VICTORIAN PAINTING HIGHLIGHTS THE PERENNIAL PROBLEM OF THE DESCREPANCY BETWEEN RICH AND POOR.

building with earth walls at Glapton in Nottinghamshire, demolished in the 1950s, had originally been a medieval cruck barn, but some time around the beginning of the seventeenth century part of it was turned into a house with hall, parlour and cross-passage.

In an attempt to control the proliferation of rural labourers' homes, an Act 'against the erecting and maintaining of cottages' was passed in 1589. According to the terms of this Act, the local Justices of the Peace had to authorize the building of a cottage, which was defined as 'a little house newly built, that hath not four acres of land to it'. This was not out of any concern for unplanned development in the rural landscape, but because of fears that the occupants of such cottages would be unable to support themselves. The notion that workshy itinerants lurked behind every hedge and in every ditch in the English countryside was a popular fear: all parts of the kingdom, said an Act of 1572, are 'presently with rogues, vagabonds, and sturdy beggars exceedingly pestered, by means whereof daily happeneth horrible murders, thefts and other outrages'. Allowing these sturdy beggars to build themselves cottages on the waste might seem a logical idea, just the thing to encourage them to settle down, get a job, start a family. But the 1572 Act, as well as providing for branding, whipping and imprisoning beggars, established the principle of compulsory taxation for the support of the poor. Justices and other officers were told that they 'shall by their good discretions tax and assess all and every the inhabitants, dwelling in all and every city, borough, town, village, hamlet and place known . . . to such weekly charge as they and every of them shall weekly contribute towards the relief of the said poor people . . .'. Although subsequent legislation directed those unable to support themselves to work, and overseers were empowered to buy 'a convenient stock of flax, hemp, wool, thread, iron and other necessary ware and stuff' to enable them to do so, it was nevertheless clear that the presence of poor people in the parish could cost money. Landless, or virtually landless, cottagers were a particularly bad risk – Francis Bacon, for instance, reckoned them to be no more than 'housed beggars'.

The result was a reluctance to allow anyone without clear means of support to build a cottage, or even to move into an existing one. In 1618 the parish officers of Eldersfield, a village just inside the Worcestershire border and a few miles north of Gloucester, set down some of the problems they were faced with:

> There are divers poor people in the said parish which are a great charge. Giles Cooke, not of our parish, married a widow's daughter within our parish, which widow is poor and lives in a small cottage, which is like to be a charge. Joan Whiple had lived 40 years and upward in the parish with a brother, as a servant to him; and now that she has grown old and weak he has put her off to the parish; she was taken begging within the parish and sent to Teddington [about ten miles east of Eldersfield], where she said she was born, but that parish has sent her back again. Elzander Man, born in Forthampton, in the county of Gloucester, married a wife within the parish,

who was received by her mother till she had two children; the said wife is now
dead, and he is gone into Gloucestershire and has left his children to the keep-
ing of the parish.

The list of grievances goes on. Thomas Jones has left his wife and two children, and the parish wants to send them after him. Francis Gatfield has moved on, leaving a child as a charge on the parish and some goods and money with his brother – can the officers either force the brother to take the child, or seize the goods as a contribution towards its upkeep?

But against this tale of woe can be set another, also of 1618, that gives the other side of the story. A petition presented to the Justices of Wiltshire for permission to settle in the parish of Stockton, about halfway between Salisbury and Warminster, shows that the policy of refusing a cottage to a bad risk could have potentially tragic consequences. The petitioner was born and brought up in Stockton and had spent most of his life in service there. He has, he says, 'taken great pains for my living all my time since I was able'. He has recently married 'with an honest young woman', but the parish would not allow him to bring her to live at Stockton, saying that any child of the marriage was likely to end up a charge on the poor rate. His petition reads:

> *Then I took a house in Bewdley, and there my wife doth yet dwell and in*
> *confines thereabouts, and I send or bring my wife the best relief I am able,*
> *and now the parish of Bewdley will not suffer her to dwell there for doubt*
> *of further charge. Right worshipful, I most humbly crave your good aid and*
> *help in this my distress, or else my poor wife and child are like to perish with-*
> *out the doors.*

The petitioner ends by pleading that the Justices should order the parish officers to permit him to have a house in the village of his birth 'to bring my wife and child unto, that I may help them the best I can'.

The 1589 Act set up a system of licensing cottages. Those built without the necessary authorization could be pulled down, and their occupants evicted. Even when there was no local opposition, it was still necessary to secure approval, as Thomas Rodger, a ploughwright of Fornham All Saints, a village a mile or so outside Bury St Edmunds, did in 1598. Having nowhere else to live, he asked Sir Thomas Kitson's permission to enclose an eighth of an acre of the village common next door to Kitson's land so he could build himself 'a cottage or poor dwelling-place' there. Rodger's plea was endorsed by eleven of his fellows, and Kitson not only granted his request but provided a load of timber and two loads of bricks towards the house. The price was that the ploughwright had to agree that on his death or that of his wife the new cottage should go to 'another of his quality or otherwise as best shall please Sir Thomas or his next successors to dispose or appoint there'. So Kitson managed to encroach on the common by the back door.

You shall dispose of your beds in such sort as that they may be in the midst of your garden, giving and allowing unto your turnips the largest room and next to them the coleworts, and unto them you shall join the space for great turnips of both sorts, and that of so much ground as would make two of the former.

After these floors you shall make a path of three foot breadth, after which you shall prepare other floors by themselves for spinach, beets, orach, rocket, parsley and sorrel. Again you shall make another path of other three feet, and on the further side you shall quarter out a bed for leeks and chives and join thereunto two other for onions and chibols and for garlick, scallions and carrots. By the side of the floors you shall make out a path of three feet and a half, and after it you shall make many floors for slips to be set upon as well for the maintaining of a plot for sweet flowers, as also for your borders, and yet further, for your winter pot-herbs. And it will be good to this end to prepare a bed for sage, and another for hyssop, one for thyme, and another for marjoram, and another for lavendar, and another for rosemary, and another for southernwood and another for small cypress. Again, one for sa-vory, for hyssop, costmary, basil, spike, balm, pennyroyal and one of camomile for to make seats and a labyrinth.

It shall be good also for necessity sake (for it concerneth the good housewife to know many remedies for diseases, and you must not doubt but that I myself have learned many remedies from the experiments and observation of those sorts of women) to shape out below, or in the further end of the kitchen garden, near to the enclosed ground for fruits, certain beds for physic herbs, as for valerian, milfoil, asparagus, mugwort, asarabacca, houseleek, patience, mercury pellitory, nicotiana, and other such like.

In such place as the sun shineth upon at noon, you shall provide your beds somewhat raised, and well mingled with earth and horse dung, and you shall let them rest sometime before they be sown. In one of which floors you shall sow, in the increase of the moon of March, your seed of lettuce and purslane (for they will be grown as soon being sowed in March as in April) for to set them again in their floors, when they be sprung up half a finger.

In this same bed you may put the seed of pimpernel, hartshorn, prick-madam, and sorrel of England, and other sorts for salads, all thick and hand over head, one among another, to separate and set at large by themselves when they be grown. Look very well to your seeds, that they be not too old, that they be winnowed and clean, that they be moist and oily, but not mouldy; and by the edges of this bed, the breadth of two hands, you shall sow artichokes. You shall also make a bed for fine herbs, which in winter serve for the pot, being kept dry and for slips for the garden of flowers, as are garden balm, basil, costmary, thyme, hyssop, savory, marjoram and sage . . .

And for fear of flying fowl and birds, cast thorns very thick upon your beds; and, if they be sown in the increase of the moon in February, for to have them the sooner to grow, yea though it be in March, yet spread upon the thorns straw, and such as is bright, and let it be thick, that so it may the better defend them from the danger of the frosts; which if you perceive to be great, as it falleth out some years, spread over them, in-stead of straw, old or whole mats, and yet in such manner as that they may not lie pressing of the earth, thereby to oppress and keep down that which would spring and grow up. Or for a more perfect surety, both to preserve your seeds in growing, and to maintain such as are grown, how under soever their natures be, from all manner of frosts, storms, or colds, which either the winter or spring can any way produce, you shall take half-rotten horse litter, and with it lightly cover all your herbs, seeds, or whatsoever else you fear the sharpness of the winter may annoy.

For besides that it is a defence and covering against the bitterness of all weathers, it hath also in it a certain warm quality, which nourisheth and strengtheneth the plants, and makes them more forward than otherwise they would be by diverse weeks. Besides, it keepeth your herbs from running into the ground, and hiding their heads in the winter season, and as if they were comforted with a continual spring, keeps them fresh and green, and fit for your use at all times . . .

All seeds which are for the store of the kitchen garden, must be sown and removed in the increase of the moon, as namely, from the first day unto the sixth; for those that are sown in the decrease, they either come up slowly, or else they be nothing worth. Besides that, although you sow in the increase of the moon, it sometime falleth out, that notwithstanding your seed be fat, full, make a white flower, and be nothing corrupted or hurt, yet some evil constellation (which the gardeners do call the course of the heavens) do hinder them that they profit not, nor yet thrive any thing at all . . .

Coleworts and spinach of all sorts, white succory, garlic, leeks, and onions, are sown in autumn, and lie all winter. Coleworts, rocket, cresses, coriander, chervil, turnips, radishes, parsnips, carrots, fennel and other herbs, whose roots are good in pottage, are sown in autumn and in the spring . . . Lettuce, sorrel, purslane, cucumbers, gourds, savory, hartshorn, trick-madam, beets, and other tender herbs, as also artichokes, are sown in the spring; and for the most part also those of March and April grow more early than those of February, according to the diversity of the time . . .

Notwithstanding that the nature of the ground, the mildness of the air, favourable furtherance of the heavens, and the age of the seed, do cause seeds to hasten the more, or to be the flower in springing out of the bosom of their mother and nurse the earth . . . yet every seed hath a cetain time to manifest itself in, whereof we must have due regard.

FROM MAISON RUSTIQUE OR THE COUNTRY FARM, BY CHARLES ESTIENNE, TRANSLATED BY RICHARD SURFLEET AND REVISED BY GERVASE MARKHAM, 1616.

The fact that Sir Thomas Kitson gave brick and timber towards the building of Thomas Rodger's cottage implies a substantial house, and certainly far beyond the rickety – and rather temporary – hovel of the Middle Ages. But how much had things really changed for the ordinary labourer by the end of the sixteenth century? Gentry houses were being built in more durable materials. 'The ancient manors and houses of our gentlemen', said William Harrison, 'are yet and for the most part of strong timber . . . Howbeit such as are lately builded are commonly either of brick or hard stone.' And in his 1602 *Survey of Cornwall*, the pioneering topographer Richard Carew, after describing local cottages of the previous century as having 'walles of earth, low thatched roofes, few partitions, no planchings or glasse windows, and scarcely any chimnies, other than a hole in the wall to let out the smoke', went on to note that 'now most of these fashions are universally banished, and the Cornish husbandman conformeth himself with a better supplied civilitie'. Yet sixteen years later Robert Reyce's *Breviary of Suffolk* painted a picture of the typical East Anglian cottage that was not so far removed from its medieval ancestor:

> *The mean person and the poor cottager thinks he doth very well if he can compass in his manner of building to raise his frame low, cover it with thatch, and to fill his widepanels (after they are well splinted and bound) with clay or culm enough well tempered, over which it may be some of more ability, both for warmth, continuance, and comeliness, to bestow a cast of hair, lime, and sand made into mortar and laid thereon, rough or smooth as the owner pleaseth.*

As always in discussions about the cottage, the problem is one of definition. Very few buildings that contemporaries would have called cottages survive from the sixteenth and seventeenth centuries. Those that we would not hesitate to describe as such have usually been redefined or redesignated as they have slipped down the social scale, or have been converted from other uses. For example, take the picturesque row of small cottages known as Arlington Row, in the pretty village of Bibury in Gloucestershire. Built in local stone with stone roofs and ten bays of cruck trusses, they date from the late fourteenth century, or rather, the structure of the building itself dates from the fourteenth century, when it was probably a monastic sheephouse. It was converted into cottages some 250 years later to accommodate outworker weavers who were supplying cloth for fulling at the local mill. The famous Almshouses at Moretonhampstead, fronted by an eleven-bay open arcade of granite, were originally a late-medieval hospital; the building was converted to house eight people in 1637 (and again in 1938 to become two dwellings).

In many parts of the country, the word 'cottage' had a distinct social and economic rather than architectural meaning. An existing building could be redefined simply as a result of the occupant's status, without any structural changes being made at all. An example of how this worked in practice is provided by a 1677 petition to the local justices of the peace by the churchwardens and overseers of the poor in Bramford, near Ipswich.

ARLINGTON ROW, BIBURY, GLOUCESTESHIRE, 14TH CENTURY, BUIILT USING 10 BAYS OF CRUCK TRUSSES.

AS THE COST OF TIMBER ROSE AND IT BECAME MORE DIFFICULT TO
PROCURE, STONE WAS INCREASINGLY USED FOR BUILDING MATERIAL.

Because of 'the great number of poore people within the saide Towne' there was an insuf-
ficient supply of cottages to house them, as a result the parish authorities 'must be forced
to turne some Antient houses of Habitation into Cottages for the necessary Reception of
their Poore'. The court granted their request, allowing 'the house of John Brasier now in
the occupation of Nathaniell Downinge . . . to be leaten as A Cottage and soe to con-
tinewe until the Court shall otherwise order'. It also licensed a further eight houses, all
currently occupied by the poor, to be rented by the parish, and two more 'antient houses'
were similarly authorized the following year. There is no evidence that these newly des-
ignated cottages were converted or changed in any way. In fact, the churchwardens were
probably seeking to regularize an existing practice, since the paupers who would benefit
from the change in status were already in residence. The Justices' approval was of itself
enough to turn a house into a cottage.

The many smaller houses that do still survive from the sixteenth and seventeenth
centuries, and that have subsequently come to be regarded as cottages benefit from sturdier construction than their medieval predecessors. (This, of course, is one reason why
they survive. No doubt there were plenty of houses that did not make use of more durable
materials and better construction techniques, but they fell down.) These structures also
show a greater diversity of building materials, with all the local variations that make the

'cottage' so attractive to modern eyes. Timber-framing continued in use for humbler and not-so-humble houses in the west, the northwest and parts of East Anglia. But forest clearances and rising timber prices meant that two of the most important reasons for building in wood – its availability and cheapness – steadily eroded, and by the seventeenth century stone was making its appearance as a material for fairly ordinary houses.

The choice of stone as a building material usually depended on a good local supply. Otherwise the high charges involved in actually transporting it could double the costs. It follows, of course, that geology plays a big part in the distribution of stone vernacular buildings. Oolitic and lias limestones, for example, both particularly suitable for building, occur naturally in a great band from Middlesbrough on the Cleveland coast down to Dorset, the 'limestone belt'. Kentish ragstone is, as its name implies, found principally in Kent; although since the main quarries were grouped around Maidstone, from where it could be carried by barge up the Medway, Kentish rag found its way by river to London (the Romans used it for the city walls), to southeast Essex and even to parts of Berkshire. In the north of England carboniferous limestone, hard rocks and slate predominate, in the southwest sandstone and gritstones. The western counties and large parts of East Anglia do not have much at all in the way of good stone, hence the relative scarcity of stone-built vernacular and the continued prevalence of timber-framed housing in these areas.

A THATCHED COTTAGE WITH STONE WALLS AND MULLIONED WINDOWS IN TEFFONT, WILTSHIRE.

The foregoing is a rather wild over-simplification of the geological map of England, leaving out as it does so much in the way of local and regional variation. Stone didn't just have to be present in order for a provincial builder to make use of it, it had to be easily quarried and easy to work. If large blocks were not readily available, walls were usually filled with random rubble, as in so many Cotswold cottages. Larger stones, roughly squared to form quoins and jambs, gave additional stability to the wall as well as offering a sense of visual completion. In other parts of the limestone belt, stone came out in thin, slate-like layers, and it was easier to lay in courses.

Stone cottages followed much the same plan-forms as their timber counterparts. They were usually only one room deep due to the problems involved in spanning any greater distance, particularly relevant when they were roofed with stone slates, which could weigh more than one ton per hundred square feet.

MARKER'S, A COB-AND-THATCH COTTAGE IN DEVON, WAS BUILT IN THE LATE MIDDLE AGES AS A SINGLE-STOREY HOUSE WITH 3 ROOMS.

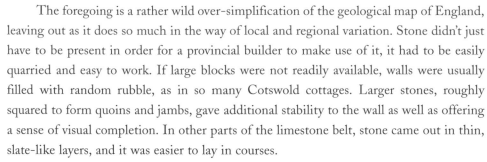

While thatch continued to be used for roofing cottages, stone slates increased in popularity during the seventeenth century. The laying of these slates called for a high degree of skill. The stone had to be split, usually at the quarry. Frost was a great help here, and it became normal to overwinter the stone before it was worked to facilitate the process. The slates varied in shape, size and thickness. The largest were hung at the bottom of the roof, and they diminished in size as they approached the ridge. They were fixed in place with pegs of oak or, more rarely, bone. Sheep's bones were occasionally used in the north of England, and Alec Clifton-Taylor tells us that at Walworth Castle in County Durham, the builders used the breast-bones of chickens. In 1688 Randle Home listed the picturesque names that builders gave to slates in different parts of the neighbourhood around Chester: haghattees, long and short, farwells, chilts, warnetts, batchlers, wivettes, rogue-why-winkest-thou, jenny-why-gettest-thou.

Beneath this great mass of haghatees and rogue-why-winkest-thous, many Tudor and Stuart villagers lived in houses that had improved considerably since the Middle Ages. Markers Cottage, a cob-and-thatch cottage on the Killerton Estate in Devon, dates from the late Middle Ages, when it was a single-storey house with three rooms and a cross-passage. The main living room – the hall – was in the centre of the house, had an open fire and was partitioned off from the other rooms by planking that reached only to about head height. In the early sixteenth century the bower or parlour beyond the hall was floored over and the partition between the two rooms extended up into the rafters, presumably to exclude smoke from the newly formed upper chamber. Soon afterwards, in about 1530, a chimney was installed on the rear wall of the hall, and the partition between hall and parlour was decorated with paintings of St Andrew, cherubs, urns and foliage. Markers clearly was not a labourer's cottage in the sixteenth century. But its evolution

MARKER'S COTTAGE WAS 'MODERNIZED' AROUND 1530 WHEN THE PAINTED

PARTITION BETWEEN HALL AND PARLOUR WAS ADDED.

shows changes typical of the period: the creation of a chamber at first-floor level and the introduction of a wall fireplace and chimney.

A smaller house of the period, of the sort that we would describe today as a cottage, might by the sixteenth century consist of three or four rooms. It was likely to be rectangular in plan, perhaps with an outshot, or lean-to, and there would be an entrance on its long side. This entrance led directly into a stone-flagged hall, still the main living area, which would be separated from the parlour by a partition of oak framing as at Markers, even if the house were built of stone. Internal walls of stone were still quite rare in humbler dwellings. A second storey was commonly reached by a simple ladder passing through a framed opening or trapdoor in the floor above, a practice that continued in some parts of the north and east of England into the nineteenth century. A slightly more sophisticated alternative was the near-vertical companionway, its steps made up of triangular timbers so that one's foot was placed beneath the step above. Staircases were rare in cottages, and they were solid rather than framed, typically placed in the recess formed by a projecting chimney breast.

The introduction of wall fireplaces and chimneys was one of the most notable developments in rural housing and it must have made a tremendous difference to living conditions. Although we take for granted as history the open hearth, with the smoke of its fire escaping, or not escaping, through holes in the wall or roof, the reality – the perpetually smoky atmosphere, the soot-blackened walls and timbers – is hard to imagine. One wonders how it was possible to spend any length of time in a cottage such as that described by Bishop Hall in the passage quoted at the beginning of this chapter. The 'thatched sparres . . . furr'd with sluttish soote a whole inch thick', the smoke drifting up and out of 'the head-les barrel' (an improvement on the unframed hole in the roof) must have made day-to-day life extremely unpleasant. Daniel King, writing in 1656, remembered with some nostalgia how Cheshire farmers until the beginning of the century 'had their fire in the midst of the house, against a hob of clay, and their oxen also under the same roof'. And in perhaps the most well-known passage from *The Description of England*, William Harrison relates that of all the changes that have taken place in his Essex village within living memory, his older parishioners comment first on 'the multitude of chimneys lately erected, whereas in

THE USUAL POSITION FOR THE STAIRCASE WAS IN THE RECESS FORMED BY THE PROJECTING CHIMNEY BREAST.

HOW TO BAKE BREAD

Our *English Housewife* shall then look into her bake-house and to the making of all sorts of bread . . .

To speak first of meals for bread, they are either simple or compound; simple, as wheat, and rye; or compound, as rye and wheat mixed together; or rye, wheat and barley mixed together. And of these the oldest meal is ever the best, and yieldeth most, so it be sweet, and untainted; for the preservation whereof, it is meet that you cleanse your meal well from the bran, and then keep it in sweet vessels.

Now for the baking of bread of your simple meals, your best and principal bread is manchet, which you shall bake in this manner. First, your meal being ground upon the black stones, if it be possible, which makes the whitest flour, and bolted [sifted] through the finest

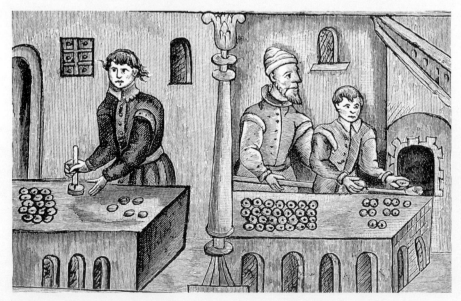

bolting cloth, you shall put it into a clean kimnel [vessel], and opening the flour hollow in the midst, put into it of the best ale barm, the quantity of three pints to a bushel of meal, with some salt to season it; then put in your liquor reasonable warm, and knead it very well together with both your hands, and through the brake [kneading machine]; or, for want thereof, fold it in a cloth, and with your feet tread it a good space together, then letting it lie an hour or thereabouts, to swell, take it forth, and mould it into manchets round and flat, scoth [score] them about the waist to give it leave to rise, and prick it with your knife in the top, and so put it into the oven, and bake it with a gentle heat.

To bake the best cheat bread, which is also simply of wheat only, you shall after your meal is dressed and bolted through a more coarse bolter than was used for your manchets, and put also into a clean tub, trough or kimnel, take a sour leaven, that is, a piece of suchlike leaven saved from a former batch, and well filled with salt, and so laid up to sour; and this sour leaven you shall break into small pieces into warm water, and then strain it; which done, make a deep hollow hole, as was before said, in the midst of your flour, and therein pour your strained liquor, then with your hand mix some part of the flour therewith, till the liquor be as thick as a pancake batter, then cover it all over with meal, and so let it lie all that night. The next morning stir it, and all the rest of the meal well together, and with a little more warm water, barm, and salt to season it with, bring it to a perfect leaven, stiff and firm. Then knead it, break it, and tread it, as was before said in the manchets, and so mould it up in reasonable big loaves, and then bake it with an indifferent good heat.

And thus according to these two examples before showed, you may bake leavened or unleavened bread whatsoever whether it be simple corn, as wheat or rye of itself; or compound grain, as wheat and rye, or wheat and barley, or rye and barley, or any other mixed white corn. Only because rye is a little stronger grain than wheat, it shall be good for you to put your water a little hotter than you did to your wheat.

For your own bread, or bread for your hind-servants, which is the coarsest bread for man's use, you shall take of barley two bushels, of peas two pecks, of wheat or rye, a peck, a peck of malt. These you shall grind all together, and dress it through a meal sieve, then putting it into a sour trough, set liquor on the fire, and when it boils, let one put in the water, and another with a mash rudder stir some of the flour with it after it hath been seasoned with salt, and so let it be till the next day, and then putting to the rest of the flour, work it up into stiff leaven, then mould it, and bake it into great loaves with a very strong heat.

Now if your trough be not sour enough to sour your leaven, then you shall either let it be longer in the trough, or else take the help of a sour leaven with your boiling water: for you must understand, that the hotter your liquor is, the less will the smell or rankness of the peas be perceived. And thus much for the baking of any kind of bread, which our *English House-wife* shall have occasion to use for the maintenance of her family.

Then in your bake-house, you shall have a fair bolting-house, with large pipes to bolt meal in, fair troughs to lay leaven in, and sweet safes to receive your bran. You shall have bolters, and meal-sieves of all sorts, both fine and coarse. You shall have fair tables to mould on, large ovens to bake in, the soles thereof, rather of one or two entire stones, than of many bricks, and the mouth made narrow, square, and easy to be close covered. As for your peels, coal-rakes, maukings, and such like, though they be necessary, yet they are of such general use they need no further relation. And thus much for a full satisfaction to all the *Husbands* and *House-wifes* of this kingdom, touching brewing, bakeing, and all whatsoever else appertaineth to either of their offices.

FROM *THE ENGLISH HOUSE-WIFE*, BY GERVASE MARKHAM, 1675.

their young days there were not above two or three, if so many, in most uplandish towns of the realm . . . but each one made his fire against a reredos in the hall, where he dined and dressed his meat'.

Things may not have been quite so bad as we imagine. The fact that Harrison's parishioners used to make their fires 'against a reredos' suggests that those fires were positioned against a wall, perhaps with smoke hoods to funnel the smoke up towards openings in the roof. And in any case, wall fireplaces were not a new phenomenon in Elizabethan England. They occur in grander houses as far back as Norman times. There were round-headed arches for these in the keeps at Colchester (1090), Rochester (1126–39) and Castle Hedingham (1130). But fireplaces begin to arrive in yeomen farmhouses during the sixteenth century, and rather than being placed in their usual position on a line with an outside wall, they also appear as a stack in the centre of the house, usually against the wall of the hall furthest from the entrance. The advantages were obvious: where there was only one fire, heat radiating from the brick stack could help to warm the rest of the house – the upper chambers that it passed through, and the parlour beyond the hall. It was not long before several fires were serviced by the one stack, so that the parlour (and occasionally the first-floor chamber or chambers) could have a fire of its own. The well-appointed cottage might also have a round bake-oven opening out of the fireplace, perhaps on one side of the chimney breast, with the staircase occupying the other. This fireplace would be spanned by a four-centred stone arch or an oak lintel.

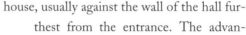

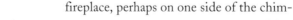

FIREPLACES BEGAN

TO ARRIVE IN YEOMAN

FARMHOUSES IN THE

16TH CENTURY.

The upper floor was either carried on wall-to-wall joists or rested on beams placed centrally across the rooms. It was usually boarded with oak or, from the seventeenth century, elm; but the boards were not always fixed, they might simply be laid across the joists. Where lime or gypsum was easily available, as it was in the East Midlands and the Cotswolds, plaster was also used as a flooring for the upper chamber. A layer of straw or reeds was laid over the joists and battened, and two or three inches of plaster applied. The undersides of the joists – the ceiling of the hall and parlour, in other words – were sometimes also plastered over, but equally they might be left exposed.

Walls were seldom carried up much more than a few feet above the level of the hall ceiling, so upper chambers were in the roof space, which made it hard to walk upright in them. It also meant that they had to be lit by a window in the end wall, a low window in the side wall, or a dormer like those so characteristic of cottages in the Cotswolds. Although glass was much more common in Elizabethan times than it had been, it was still very expensive and rarely used for the windows of cottages. Labourers had to make do with oiled paper, 'linen clothe straked across with lozenges' to simulate lattices, or nothing but boards and sacking to keep out the wind and rain.

There was an enormously diverse range and quality in Tudor and Stuart rural worker-housing, if the phrase 'worker-housing' can have any meaning for a society in which trade, wage-labour and smallscale farming could all be carried out by the same people in the same household. The two-room cottage of Bartholomew Birch, a labourer who lived in the village of Shadoxhurst a few miles outside Ashford in Kent in the 1660s, was functional but well equipped. His hall was filled with table, chairs and cooking equipment, the

THE LARGE OPEN HEARTH WITH A BAKE-OVEN BUILT INTO THE SIDE OF THE
CHIMNEY BREAST WAS A COMMON FEATURE IN RURAL COTTAGES.

FOR SOME, HAVING A FIRE IN ONE'S HEARTH AND A ROOF OVER ONE'S HEAD
WERE NO LONGER ENOUGH.

chamber above contained a bedstead for him and his wife and a truckle bed, and in the 'drinke hows' and dairy the Birches brewed their own beer and made their own butter and cheese. They owned three cows and a pig, and Bartholomew owned his own tools, timber and planks for making up simple pieces of furniture and even a gun. Yet barely habitable hovels were still commonplace, as John Taylor the 'water-poet' found when he was looking for lodgings in Hastings in 1623:

> *Within a cottage nigh, there dwells a weaver*
> *Who entertain'd as the like was never;*
> *No meat, no drink, no lodging but the floor,*
> *No stool to sit, no lock upon the door,*
> *No straw to make us litter in the night,*
> *Nor any candlestick to hold the light.*

Who can say which is more typical of the period – the busy workplace of Bartholomew Birch or the poor weaver's cottage? But the conversions and improvements made to medieval buildings during the sixteenth and seventeenth centuries, and the evidence on the ground from surviving newly built houses, imply that expectations of comfort and convenience were higher, even if many people could not hope to meet those expectations. For some, having a fire in one's hearth and a roof over one's head were no longer enough.

'Some men will have their walls plastered, some pargetted, and whitelimed, some rough cast, some pricked, some wrought with plaster of Paris.' William Horman's comments, dating from 1519, illustrate how the aesthetics of architecture were assuming a new importance in Tudor England. Form had not quite triumphed over function: there were sound practical reasons for providing a timber building with a coat of plaster, not least that it gave some protection against fire. But plaster was also used to mask different building materials and different building periods (and it still does, quite effectively, as vernacular historians know, to their cost), and as Horman points out, it presented an opportunity for modest external decoration. Pargetting, the art of creating ornamental patterns in the plaster before it was dry, became a common finish to cottages and smaller buildings all over Essex and Suffolk, and also in parts of Hertfordshire, Cambridgeshire and down into Kent. In its first, early Tudor phase it involved no more than the making of simple geometrical patterns with a pointed stick or a wooden comb, and for humbler cottages this method was still practised into the eighteenth century. But by the 1600s designs had become much more elaborate. There were panels formed by giving smooth and sometimes sculpted borders to the rough surface of the finish; simple geometrical patterns, rather like designs for knot gardens; even extremely complicated, almost baroque cartouches and scrollwork, made with moulds and templates. Running friezes scallops, herringbone and chequerwork can all be found on the cottages of Norfolk and Suffolk. In Kent examples of floral patterns in the gables of seventeenth- and early-eighteenth-century cottages still survive.

Inside the cottage, rising standards of living were also evident. Harrison's old villagers comment on

> *The great (although not general) amendment of lodging; for, said they, our fathers, yea and we ourselves also, have lain full oft upon straw pallets, on rough mats covered only with a sheet, under coverlets made of dagswain or hopharlots (I use their own terms), and a good round log under their heads instead of a bolster or pillow. If it were so that our fathers, or the good man of the house had within seven years after his marriage purchased a mattress or flock bed, and thereto a stack of chaff to rest his head upon, he thought himself to be as well lodged as the lord of the town . . . Pillows (said they) were thought meet only for women in childbed.*

Richard Carew in his *Survey of Cornwall* makes the same point, noting how things have changed since the time when Cornish cottagers had for their bed only straw and a blanket, and 'as for sheets, so much linnen cloth had not yet

17TH-CENTURY PARGETTING AT SAFFRON WALDEN, ESSEX. 'SOME MEN WILL HAVE THEIR WALLS PLASTERED, SOME PARGETTED', WROTE WILLIAM HORMAN IN 1519.

PARGETTING AS USED AT CLARE IN SUFFOLK (1473). THE TECHNIQUE

PROVIDED AN OPPORTUNITY FOR EXTERNAL DECORATION.

stepped over the narrow channel betweene them and Brittaine'. Harrison also talks of

> *the exchange of vessel, as of treen [wooden] platters into pewter, and wood-*
> *en spoons into silver or tin . . . whereas in my time, although peradventure*
> *four pounds of old rent be improved to forty, fifty, or a hundred pounds, yet*
> *will the farmer . . . [have] a fair garnish of pewter on his cupboard, with so*
> *much more in odd vessel going about the house, three or four feather beds, so*
> *many coverlids and carpets of tapestry, a silver salt, a bowl for wine, and a*
> *dozen of spoons.*

Again his observations are confirmed, this time by a ballad of 1547:

> *For they that of late did sup*
> *Out of an ashen cup*
> *Are wonderfully sprung up;*
> *That nought was worth of late,*
> *Hath now a cupboard of plate,*
> *His table furnished too*
> *With plate.*

These remarks relate not to the cottager, but to the prosperous yeoman who did quite well out of the collapse of the feudal system. Some villagers moved down the economic ladder: they fell from landholding peasant, with the opportunity to use that land to provide subsistence and some income, to landless labourer, dependent entirely on the employment market for their living. Others moved up, carried by the expansion in the wool trade. They bought their neighbours' land and left their traditional holdings for bigger farms on the outskirts of villages. Villeinage was almost extinct – almost, but not quite. When, for example, Robert Ringwood came before the justices in Norwich in 1561 to claim that Lewis Lowth was bound to him to serve as his apprentice for seven years, Lowth brought John Holdiche to swear that 'the said Lewis is a bondsman to my Lord of Norfolk's grace, and further that he was brought up in husbandry until he was twenty years old'. Ringwood's case was thrown out of court.

Changes in tenure meant land that had originally been held in villeinage was now held in one of three basic ways. A tenant could be 'at will', which meant that he only held his land for as long as his lord pleased and on his lord's terms. He might be a customary tenant, in which case his rights were protected by the 'custom of the manor' enrolled in the manorial court roll. Or, if he possessed a copy of the record, he was a copyholder. Apart from those who held their lands freehold, the village elite were the copyholders who had an 'estate of inheritance' with fine certain. When they died,

The Cheshire cheese is properly a new milk cheese. Some make these with new milk, enriched by the cream of the last milking, and others of new milk, impoverished by an addition of the skimmed milk of a preceding meal. In Cheshire their pastures are so rich, that they never find it needful to enrich their new milk, for it alone will make cheese of the richest kind that can be . . .

They are particular as to the condition of the cow; and this is a caution all farmers would do well to take from them. They find by experience, that the milk of a cow which has just calved, is not so proper as that a few days after; therefore they never take the milk of any cow for cheese till she has been milked four or five times. They use their whole store of new milk, a very little excepted, in the cheese manufacture. When the morning's milking is brought in, they strain it warm into a large tub, and put in their rennet. About four spoonfuls is the quantity they allow to as much milk as will afford a cheese of a hundred weight . . . They cover up the tub, and when it has stood half an hour they open it, and find the curd formed. They are very cautious to hit the right quantity of rennet, which no rule can determine, because of the difference in the strength; for too little does not give the curd due consistence, and too much makes the cheese bitter. After half an hour they uncover the tub, and press down the curd with a large skimming dish; and when they have pretty well cleared off the whey, they work the curd with their hands, they break it to pieces in the most perfect manner, working it a long time.

This done, supposing it for a hundred weight cheese, they add one pound of salt; this they mix thoroughly well with the curd. Then they put the curd into a wet, strong and large cheese-cloth, and when they have got the whey tolerably well drained out, they put it into the fat, or mould, for four hours, with a good pressure, putting the fat in the cheese press, and working it down pretty strongly. At the end of four hours they take it out, salt the outside, put it into a fresh wet cloth, and put it into the fat, and that into the press again. Here it is to be kept four hours more; and in the mean time a quantity of good strong brine is to be made of salt and water, and put into a large tub.

When the cheese has been four hours in the press they take it out, and put it into the tub of brine, and there let it lie eight days, all the time covered over with brine, and turned once a day. At the end of this time it is to be taken out, and laid to harden and dry. A quantity of rushes are to be cut up, and laid green on a large board. On these the cheese is to be laid when taken out of the brine, and for the first day nothing is done to it. The next morning it is to be turned and wiped with a hair cloth all over; and this is to be repeated every day for twenty days.

At the end of this time it must be removed from the bed of rushes and laid on the floor; and it is here to be taken up, and turned once in three days, and at every turning is to be rubbed, till it gets firm and hard. As this is the completing the work, it is to be managed very carefully; for if the due degree of hardness be not given at this time, the cheese will be liable to accidents in keeping.

When finished and hardened, the last thing is the rubbing it over with some butter. Half a pound of butter is proper for a cheese of a hundred weight, and this should be rubbed thoroughly in all over it, nothing more tending to preserve the rind in good condition, and keep the cheese sound.

This is the method in that famous cheese county. They have rooms built on purpose for the drying of their large cheeses, and they raise the floors several feet above the ground, to preserve them from damp. In many places they use shelves put round these rooms, instead of the floor, which I think the better method, for the cheeses are more out of the reach of damp, and they are more easily turned, and more conveniently rubbed and wiped.

A Nettle cheese is a very thin new milk cheese, with an exceeding fine and smooth coat. It differs from the common new milk cheeses more in the form and the manner of drying than in anything essential. For the drying of Cheshire cheeses... they use a bed of rushes spread evenly upon the floor of the room: in the same manner a bed of common nettles is the matter on which these cheeses are dried, and from which they receive their name; the nettles upon this occasion are to be fresh cut. And the manner of making cheese is this: let the milk of the morning's milking be taken as it comes in warm from the cows, without any addition. Let this be strained into a large pan, and let there be immediately added as

much rennet as will turn it. 'Tis then to be covered up half an hour. Then the curd is to be pressed down, and the whey skimmed off, and when thus separated the curd is to be wrought in the hands. When it is well worked it is to be put into a cheese fat and pressed to get out the whey.

From *A Compleat Body of Husbandry*, by Thomas Hale, 1758.

their heirs automatically succeeded to their land, and the lord of the manor could not do anything about it. He could not give their holdings to anyone else, nor could he increase the size of the fine to force them out. But if the entry on the court roll provided for a life-interest only or for a fine arbitrary (at the will of the lord), then the copyholder's heir had to pay what the lord asked or go. This was a common cause of complaint in the sixteenth century. Many writers lamented 'the daily oppression of copyholders, whose lords seek to bring their poor tenants almost into plain servitude and misery, daily devising new means, and seeking up all the old, how to cut them shorter and shorter, doubling, trebling, and now and then seven times increasing their fines, driving them also for every trifle to lose and forfeit their tenures . . . to the end they may fleece them yet more, which is a lamentable hearing'. A seventeenth-century ballad, *Mockbeggar Hall*, echoes the complaint:

A DARTMOOR COTTAGE. 'THE TENANT MUST GIVE A GOLDEN SUM, OR ELSE
HE IS TURNED PACKING', FROM A 17TH-CENTURY BALLAD.

Young landlords when to age they come,
Their rents they will be racking.
The tenant must give a golden sum,
Or else he is turned packing,
Great fines and double rent beside.

The push to evict was driven partly by a desire for higher rents, partly by an effort to bring land back in hand in order to capitalize on the potential revenue offered by large-scale farming. Thomas Bastard's *Chrestoleros* (1598) condemns the encloser who,

Steals away both subjects from the Queen
And men from his own country of all sorts.
Houses by three and seven and ten he razeth,
To make the common glebe his private land;
Our country cities cruel he defaceth.

But cottagers and husbandmen could not be thrown off their land willy-nilly. While the many and various differences in manorial custom provided the basis for a vast deal of litigation, the ordinary villager as often as not succeeded in asserting his rights. As a result, landowners soon began to dislike these tenures, and throughout the sixteenth century there was a general move to alter copyholds into leases.

The intricacies of tenure and the jockeying for power that lay behind them helped to confirm the shape of many an English village. As farms grew and farmers sought to emulate the more private and less communal lifestyle that was becoming fashionable among the gentry and nobility, farm labourers were moved out of their traditional lodgings in the farmhouse itself and relegated to cottages on or near the farm. More importantly, the break-up of the manorial system created two types of village: the closed community, in which one landowner dominated or completely controlled the holdings and hence the houses of everybody in the settlement; and the open village, where no single landlord held sway, and where squatters could still erect cottages on the waste and speculators could buy up land and build low-cost housing to rent among the leasehold and freehold properties that already existed.

The scale of land transfers may go some way towards explaining the fact that the village was a much less stable community than we used to think. Recent studies of individual villages in the sixteenth and seventeenth centuries have shown that social structures changed quite dramatical-

THE FRONTISPIECE TO JOHN WORLIDGE'S *SYSTEMA AGRICULTURAE*, 1668, SHOWS A SCHEME FOR A TYPICAL ESTATE.

ly over relatively short periods of time. At Earls Colne in Essex, for example, only twenty-three out of 274 pieces of property listed in a rental roll for 1677 were still in the hands of the families who had them in 1589. And the parish records of Cogenhoe in Northamptonshire show that over half the 180 people living there in 1628 had arrived within the previous ten years. As J. A. Sharpe remarks in *Early Modern England*, the early modern village may have been a face-to-face society, but the faces were constantly changing.

The rapid turnover of families and individuals, while it clearly varied from one part of the country to another, suggests that the bonds that tied villagers together into a cohesive unit, the sense of common purpose that was such a feature of the feudal system, were loosening during the Tudor and Stuart periods. Certainly there was an increasing social stratification within the rural community. The rise of the yeoman farmer as an important member of village society, the consolidation of landholdings and the consequent increase in the numbers of landless labourers, all helped to create a class system of sorts. The village was still the primary unit of rural life, and the medieval mistrust of 'strangers', 'foreigners' – anyone, in fact, who was unknown – remained. But the social deference that had been a privilege enjoyed by the nobility and gentry was filtering down to the farmer and the merchant. Most ordinary cottagers, of course, had neither the time nor the inclination to muse over the ins and outs of changing settlement patterns or the ramifications of social class. They were concerned with getting by, getting work, getting on with their neighbours, with all the emotional minutiae in daily life.

Generalizations about family life are dangerous at any time. One only has to think for a moment about one's own friends and acquaintances to realize that there are so many exceptions to any rule about the nature of sexual or filial relationships that the rule itself is unworkable. The lack of evidence about the intimate lives of cottager-dwellers makes the process even more difficult. We know that the nuclear family was the norm as it had been in the Middle Ages. As far as we can tell, marriages among all but the propertied classes were made for love rather than convenience. Sometimes the union worked, and sometimes it didn't. When it didn't, the labourer or his wife could terminate the arrangement not by divorce, but by the simple expedient of desertion. Remarriage after the disappearance of one partner – bigamy, in other words – was quite common among the poorer classes. Wives were expected to obey their husbands, and children were expected to respect their parents, and these concepts were reinforced by the Church, especially by post-Reformation Protestant ideology, and perhaps more importantly by peer-group pressure. A villager's reputation among his or her peers mattered, a fact witnessed to by the various forms of community action designed to punish anyone who deviated from socially accepted behaviour. Sharpe cites several cases of scolds who were presented before the Archdeacon of Durham in 1600, such as Mary Taylor, who ' by her evill & rayling temper misusethe & formethe dissension amonge hir neighbours', and Isabel Remission, 'a verrey idle scolde & a disquieter of her neighbours with malicious speeches'.

Recourse to law was only one way of correcting what was seen as deviant behaviour. Community pressure could often be more effective. In the Great Hall at Montacute, a late-Elizabethan country house in Somerset, a large early-seventeenth-century plaster panel shows a man being beaten by his wife for taking a drink while minding the baby. The scene is witnessed by a neighbour, and as a result the rest of the village enacts a form of public humiliation in which one villager, impersonating the hen-pecked husband, sits astride a pole and is carried round the village to the accompaniment of music and shouting. 'The skimmington ride', also known as 'riding the stang', was common in England, Scotland, Scandinavia, even in Spain, according to Hofnagel's *Views of Seville* (1591), and is referred to in Sir Walter Scott's *Fortunes of Nigel* and Thomas Hardy's *The Mayor of Casterbridge*, suggesting it was still practised in outlying areas in the nineteenth century. How effective it was in teaching a husband to occupy his 'proper' role as head of the household is hard to judge. The butt of one such ride, in Leeds in 1667, clearly did not see the funny side – when the crowd reached his house he shot two of them dead.

AN IDEALIZED 19TH-CENTURY VIEW, SHOWING THE HUGE HEARTH THAT
WAS AT THE CENTRE OF DOMESTIC LIFE.

Sexual morality is another area where the pressure of one's neighbours enforced accepted codes of behaviour. To judge from what documentary evidence there is (parish records, for example, suggest that around twenty per cent of all women were already pregnant when they married) and from the completely open living arrangements in most cottages (where parents and children almost invariably occupied the same room), one might think that promiscuity was rife and that sex was a public act. But one sexual partner was the norm. Premarital pregnancies usually occurred between couples who had already exchanged vows – promises to marry, in other words – and most labouring people viewed this as sanction enough for the sexual act. Where illegitimate births did occur, they were often the result either of a promise of marriage being reneged on or – one area where illicit sex *was* quite common – the seduction of a servant-girl.

The Church did all it could to regulate sexual conduct, and presentations to consistory courts suggest that informing on the transgressors was one means of regulating moral behaviour within the community:

> *Thomas Sturman was reported by his wife that he and Mary Rayner did live together incontinently.*

> *Thomas Campion was presented for begetting his wife with Child before they were married.*

> *Wee present Elizabeth – singleton of this parish for committing fornication with one John Tomlin as is supposed and as the common fame goeth.*

As far as the time and the place for sex are concerned, there is little evidence to go on. Few people were obliging enough to follow the example of Pepys, who records his couplings in detail, or Robert Hooke, who marked down in his diaries whenever he had an orgasm (sometimes alone, sometimes with his niece). But it seems unlikely that most couples were content to do their coupling in front of their children. Makeshift screens of sacking and rags were often placed between parents' beds and those of their offspring. Otherwise, both darkness and open fields provided plenty of opportunities for more intimate and less public sex.

On the death of his father in March 1659, twenty-three-year-old George Vernon inherited the family estates in Derbyshire and Staffordshire. Chief among these was the manor of Sudbury on the border of those two counties. A manor house built by George's great-grandmother in the early 1600s stood back from the lane that ran through the village. In front of it and scattered around the fields were a motley collection of cottages and farmsteads, most of them, like the manor house itself, built of timber with wattle and daub panels. The church was probably the only building of stone.

16TH-CENTURY HOUSE IN COLCHESTER. GLASS, STILL EXPENSIVE AT THE TIME, WAS RARELY USED FOR COTTAGES.

The following year George made a lucrative marriage (the first of three), and immediately embarked on a large-scale building programme. He decided to replace the manor house with a much more imposing hall, and as a prelude to this he swept away the old cottages that obstructed the view across his land. A great avenue of trees stretched out from his new house, cutting a swathe through a landscape that had once been dotted with labourers' homes. In rebuilding both the hall and the village the young squire used red brick, dug in the fields around his estate and moulded and fired in makeshift clamps or kilns on site. For the next twenty years or so Sudbury was one great building plot. Itinerant gangs of brickmakers and masons came and went, and villagers were paid to clear rubble and carry building materials and fuel for the clamps. Neat groups and terraces of two-, three- and four-roomed cottages replaced many of the single-storeyed, one-room hovels. A new village inn replaced the old one. Even outlying farms on the estate were rebuilt.

THE EAST AND SOUTH-EAST HAD BEEN IMPORTING FLEMISH BRICKMAKERS AND KNOWHOW SINCE THE 16TH CENTURY.

Sudbury was not the first settlement to be reconstructed in brick. With its close trading links to the Low Countries, for example, East Anglia had been importing Flemish brickmakers since the sixteenth century. Nor was it the first purpose-built estate village. But it is a symbol of the last stages of the Great Rebuilding as well as a foretaste of things to come. In closed villages like Sudbury, where one individual owned the majority of the housing, that person's desire to control and regulate the surrounding landscape meant that the cottage was becoming subject to a landlord's tastes as well as his agricultural interests. It was only a matter of time before the cottage began to play a more active role in the landscape, an art object as well as a home.

CHAPTER III

Miserable Hovels

1690~1790

Where plenty smiles, alas! She smiles for few.

GEORGE CRABBE, *THE VILLAGE*, 1783

Robert Hawes was a bricklayer. He lived in what was probably a one-room cottage in Roxwell, Essex, and he died in 1691. An inventory of Robert's possessions was taken by his neighbours after his death. This was a means of assessing the value of his estate – a legal requirement from the sixteenth century to the nineteenth – and had to be produced when probate was granted or, if the person concerned died intestate, when letters of adminstration were issued.

Robert Hawes' inventory shows that he owned a feather bed with bolster, coverlet and blanket; some linen, including two towels, a table cloth and 'two payer of olde sheets'; nine pounds in weight of pewter; a leather bottle and a bucket; an old hutch (a chest used for storing clothes) and a cupboard; a copper, some working tools and his 'wearing apparell'. The whole lot was valued at £3.17s.3d. A note added to the inventory showed that he did not actually own the copper after all – he had borrowed it.

Slightly better off was John Day the elder, who came from nearby Highwood. John was a carpenter, and his worldly goods and house seem to have been rather more substantial. His inventory shows that he lived in a typical artisan's cottage of the early eighteenth century with four main rooms – a living hall with a fireplace and a parlour with a bed, both on the ground floor, and two more bedchambers above.

But Day was by no means prosperous, if the appraisers who drew up the inventory are to be relied upon. The parlour adjoining the hall contained, along with a couple of chests and a small table, 'one indeferant bed' and '2 sorry old chairers'. The parlour chamber – the room above – boasted more chests and trunks, and 'one sorry bed'. And the hall chamber next door had more cupboards and chests, and 'two beds with what belongs to them very mean'. The outbuildings, which probably stood as a single-storey block added on at the back of the cottage, were better equipped. There was a cheesepress in the dairy, two twenty-seven-gallon casks in the buttery, and a copper, a brass kettle and four tubs for brewing beer in the brewhouse. Day also kept two cows grazing on the local common, he had four pairs of sheets to Hawes's two (one pair for each bed, presumably), and the value of his goods came to the grand total of £15.6s.

Still higher up the social scale comes John Webb, a yeoman of Roxwell, who died in 1690. Webb's house is altogether

As rural labourers rarely kept written records, little is known

of their private, daily lives apart from statistics.

more spacious than John Day's. In addition to a living hall and a parlour, there is a separate kitchen, two butteries, a malthouse and a dairy, and no fewer than five bedchambers – three above the main rooms on the ground floor, a fourth over the dairy and 'a little chamber over the entry', presumably a porch room. Webb clearly ran a fair-sized smallholding: a spade, a shovel, a mattock, an axe, a bill and 'other implements of husbandrie' lay in the kitchen, while his livestock included a horse harness and two carts, two cows, eight ewes with their lambs and two pigs. He was also growing corn, which was valued at the time of his death at £13.13s.

Inventories can build a surprisingly vivid picture of rural existence during the sev-

UNTIL WELL INTO VICTORIAN TIMES, MOST OF INFORMATION ON COTTAGERS COMES FROM THOSE WHO

EITHER IDEALIZED THEM OR THOSE WHO REGARDED THEM WITH INDIFFERENCE OR CONTEMPT.

enteenth and eighteenth centuries, helping to bring alive men and women who would otherwise be no more than names in parish registers, their lives unrecorded and forgotten. One of the most frustrating problems in exploring the history of life in the English cottage is a lack of information about individuals. Until well into the nineteenth century – and unlike the landed classes in their country houses – the rural labourer rarely kept records, letters, accounts, diaries. Apart from the physical evidence of their homes, most of which have changed beyond recognition, the only information we have is filtered through the writings of those who did.

Much of that information is partial and, to modern sensibilities, callously unfeeling.

A strict sense of hierarchy, unmitigated by those feelings of philanthropy and moral oblig-ation which would become such a feature of attitudes towards the rural poor in Victorian times, meant that individual cottage-dwellers rarely figured in contemporary documents for the simple reason that they did not matter. Travellers, topographers and excursionists were busy exploring England in the late seventeenth and eighteenth centuries, marvelling at great country houses, manufactories and natural curiosities. Yet in their journals and diaries, rural worker-housing and its occupants provoked little more than a patronizing disdain and a smug sense of superiority. For example, the intrepid but scarcely empathet-ic Celia Fiennes, while touring the Lake District on horseback in the 1690s, expressed surprise at the condition of rural housing:

> Here I came to villages of sad little hutts made up of drye walls, only stones
> piled together and the roofs of same slatt; there seemed to be little nor noe tun-
> nells for their chimneys and have no morter or plaister within or without; for
> the most part I tooke them at first sight for a sort of houses or barns to fodder
> cattle in, not thinking them to be dwelling houses, they being scattering hous-
> es here one there another.

But while she comments that such sad little huts 'must needs be very cold dwellings', she dismisses the cottagers' sufferings with the remark that 'it shews something of the lazyness of the people'. Her chief concern is for what she can get to eat, as she bemoans the fact that bread and butter, cheese and beer are all one can obtain in these villages.

A lack of compassion for the rural poor was by no means unusual. In 1746 Sir Frederick Eden asserted that 'There seems to be just reason to conclude that the miseries of the labouring Poor arise, less from the scantiness of their income (however much the philanthropists might wish it to be increased) than from their own improvidence and unthriftiness.' And during a tour of Bedfordshire at the end of the eighteenth century, John Byng noted in his diary that he gave some loose change to 'two human male beings, whose nakedness was not conceal'd by rags . . . They seem'd to be about 12 or 14 years of age. Meat and fuel being unknown, but few children can be rear'd; and who would strive to rear them? The sooner they are starv'd the better.'

In the literature of the period, cottage-dwellers are a class, a separate race, perhaps even a social problem, but they rarely emerge from con-temporary documents as individual personalities. We know, for exam-ple, that in the 1680s, when Sir John Brownlow was building Belton House in Lincolnshire, he employed local villagers; Brownlow's building accounts contain payments to them for clearing the site and gathering gorse and bracken as fuel for his brick kilns. We know, again from build-ing accounts, that when George Vernon moved the old village of Sudbury in Derbyshire in the 1660s as a prelude to building his new Hall, he also employed his cottagers as casual labour. But we have nothing beyond names, the Johns, Alices, Samuels and Thomases. We know who Brownlow and Vernon married, we know the birthdays of their children, we know the circumstances of their deaths; we can still see the great houses they lived in, the paintings and furniture they bought to fill them. But apart from a few chance entries in ledgers and parish registers, the cottagers who lived, worked and died in their villages remain an enigma.

Robert Hawes, John Webb and John Day, on the other hand, come down to us as real people. Hawes did not even have a stool to sit on in his hovel. The bed in Day's parlour chamber had a linsey-woolsey mattress case or tick (described by the inventorist as a 'linciwolcy teeke'). Standing in Webb's dairy, as his neighbours summed up his goods three centuries ago, were 'ten little cheeses'. The surviving catalogues of what lay in their homes, and in the homes of thousands of ordinary men and women like them, may be incomplete. They were, after all, made by semi-literate neighbours, and some took the job more seriously than others. But they do provide us with an intriguing insight

into the day-to-day lives of individual cottagers in a way that the accounts of upper-class tourists do not.

Let's indulge in a little speculation. John Day's cottage in Highwood is, we know, two storeys high, probably with a single-storey extension behind it. We have no idea how long it has been standing by the time of Day's death, but we can assume that local materials were used. Brick was still quite rare for the construction of an artisan's cottage in the 1720s, and in stoneless Essex the likelihood is that Day's house was timber-framed with a cladding of either weather-board or plaster. The roof was perhaps thatched.

We would enter directly into the hall, as the inventorists did. This was the largest room in the house, and served as principal living area and perhaps also as kitchen, although the buttery may have taken over some of that function. The walls and floor are

BRINGING IN THE HARVEST, *c.* 1725. THE 18TH-CENTURY ESTATE OWNER

WAS EAGER TO ADVANCE 'AGRICULTURAL IMPROVEMENT'.

bare. There are no curtains at the windows here or in any of the other rooms. The fireplace – the only one in the cottage – has a simple iron fire shovel and tongs. The fire is laid directly on the brick hearth rather than being raised above it (there is no mention of firedogs or fire basket), and wood is burning there – faggots and logs were the fuel in general use in Essex at the time. There is also almost certainly a brick-lined oven, either next to the fireplace, or possibly out in the buttery.

There are three spits, probably hanging on a rack over the fire. The fact that these are described in the inventory as 'small' suggests they are used for game rather than for joints of meat. A typical spit of the period consisted of no more than a long iron shaft, flattened in the middle and rounded at the ends so that it could be turned smoothly. One of those ends had a grooved driving wheel for a pulley or, more likely, a simple handle, the other was spiked. There is no mention of spit racks (a pair of iron stands with a series of hooks to allow the cook to raise and lower the spits above the fire), and it is unlikely that a family of Day's status would possess any of the more elaborate machinery used for turning spits – dogwheels or weight-driven spit jacks. So perhaps the hearth was equipped with fixed spit hooks which, since they were not portable, would be of no interest to the inventorists.

A nice domestic touch is Day's warming pan, hanging by the fireplace. This long-handled shallow pan – shiny copper reproductions of which found their way into thousands of middle-class homes in the 1930s and 1940s – would be filled with hot embers from the fire and smoothed over the old carpenter's bed to warm it at night.

The furniture in the hall consists of 'one long table, 6 joynt stooles, two other small tables, 4 old chairs, one cuberd'. Did Day make any of them himself? He was a carpenter, after all. They were probably solid and unadorned. Oak, ash, yew and elm were the common woods. The six pewter dishes and six plates were the usual tableware for the period.

Unusually for an artisan, John Day possesses a clock, although we have no way of knowing what type – weight-driven, spring-driven and pendulum clocks were all in use in the 1720s. It can hardly have been much of a showpiece: the whole contents of the hall, clock included, were valued at a mere £2. 10s. By way of comparison, Margaret Haward, a neighbouring widow and small farmer who died in 1729, four years after Day, owned a long-case clock which alone was valued at £4. 5s. But then she was comparatively

---

JOHN DAY THE ELDER, OF HIGHWOOD IN WRITTLE, CARPENTER.
16 MARCH 1725/6.

In the hall
One long table, 6 joynt stooles, two other small tables, 4 old chairs, one cuberd, fire shovel and tongs, 3 small spits, 6 peuter dishes, 6 pleats, one bras candle stick, som other small implements, one clock, one worming pan, £2 10s.

In the parler
One indeferant bed, & bedsted with all belonging too it, one chest of drauers, one pres cubard, one small table, 2 sorry old chairers, £1 4s.

In the buttre
Two half hogsheds, one iron porridg pots, 7s.

In the dary
One chespres, one stand, 3 woden trays, and a few earthen pans, and other small implements, 7s.

In the brewhouse
One small copper, four tubs, one bras cettle, other small things, £1 5s.

In the chamber over the parler
One sorry bed with a linciwolcy teeke, and bedsted, one small table, three hutchis, 2 truncks, £1 10s.

In the hall chamber
Two beds with what belongs to them very mean, one cubbard, 2 hutchis, £1 10s.

Two cows that are kept upon the Commans, £4.
Waring clothis and mony in his purs, £1 10s.
Linlin
4 pair of sheets, 6 napkins, 3 board cloths, £1 3s.
£15 6s.

well-to-do – she owned 'tea potts & cups', a rarity in Essex at the time.

Although John Day owned a brass candlestick, most of the artificial light in his home would have been provided by rushlights, which were the chief form of lighting in cottages well into the nineteenth century. Rush-holders, rather like clothes-pegs on stands, were probably among the unspecified 'other small implements' that follow the 'one bras candle stick' in the inventory, along with a tinder-box. In 1775 Gilbert White gave a detailed description of how the rushes were prepared in his *Natural History of Selborne*:

> *Decayed labourers, women, and children, make it their business to procure and prepare them. As soon as they are cut, they must be flung into water, and kept there, for otherwise they will dry and shrink, and the peel will not run. At first a person would find it no easy matter to divest a rush of its peel or rind, so as to leave one regular, narrow, even rib from top to bottom that may support the pith; but this like other feats, soon become familiar even to children . . . When these [rushes] are thus prepared, they must lie out on the grass to be bleached, and take the dew for some nights, and afterwards be dried in the sun.*

> *Some address is required in dipping these rushes in scalding fat or grease; but this knack also is to be attained by practice. The careful wife of an industrious Hampshire labourer obtains all her fat for nothing; for she saves the scummings of her bacon-pot for this use: and, if the grease abounds with salt, she causes the salt to precipitate to the bottom, by setting the scummings in a warm oven . . . If men that keep bees will mix a little wax with the grease, it will give it a consistency, and render it more cleanly, and make the rushes burn longer; mutton-suet would have the same effect.*

According to White, a good rush, two feet, four inches long, would burn for nearly an hour with 'a good clear light'. It was cheap, too. He calculated that a dipped rush cost one eleventh of a farthing, and that a pound and a half of rushes would supply a family all year round. The constant stench of burning bacon fat or mutton suet, on the other hand, is something that modern sensibilities would find rather repellent.

The second room on the ground floor of John Day's cottage, probably reached through a simple studwork partition, is the parlour. The parlour was in a state of transition in vernacular housing of the late seventeenth and early eighteenth centuries. In grander households, such as that of yeoman John Webb, it had become a second living room – *his* parlour contained two small tables, two rush chairs and a set of pewter tableware. But in others, Day's included, it was still the main bedchamber. This was where John would have slept in the 'one indeferant bed', probably a freestanding affair consisting of a solid rectangular frame with posts at each corner. Clothes were kept in the 'prescubard', the equivalent of a wardrobe with two doors and simple mouldings. There was also a chest of drawers. Other storage in the cottage came in the form of two trunks and five 'hutchis', all kept in the two upstairs bedchambers, which may have occupied the roofspace. We can only guess at what they contained. 'Trunk' implies a wooden, leather-covered box with a domed lid, which usually held bedding or linen. A hutch was a smaller version of a chest and, as previously mentioned, was normally used for storing clothes.

The single-storey block behind the cottage, reached via the buttery with its cast-iron porridge pot, consisted of a dairy and a brewhouse. Both brewing and cheesemaking were common practices with cottage-dwellers well into the nineteenth century. The cheese-press that stood in the dairy, used for consolidating the curd after it had been placed in cheese moulds, would have been either weighted down with stones or, if Day had one of the more modern presses, equipped with a wooden screw.

ԾՆ ԾՆ ԾՆ

It used to be said that the eighteenth century witnessed an agrarian revolution on a scale to match the industrial revolution; that agricultural improvements – Jethro Tull's seed-drill, Thomas Coke's progressive farming methods in Norfolk, the new stockbreeding techniques introduced by Robert Bakewell – showed landowners the need for larger farms; and that this in turn led to a wave of enclosures that dispossessed the rural small-holder, drove him from his cottage to seek work in the emergent industries of the towns, and created the foundations of the urban working class. The truth is not so simple.

There was no dramatic agrarian revolution, rather a gradual adoption and modifica-tion of agricultural practices that had been developed elsewhere, mainly in the Low Countries, during the previous century. As a result, there is evidence that larger estates were tending to swallow up smaller holdings over the course of the eighteenth century, but nowhere near as much as was once thought. It has been estimated that in 1690, the gentry and aristocracy between them already owned between sixty and seventy per cent of land in England. One hundred years later this had risen – but only as high as seventy to seventy-five per cent.

There is also evidence that patterns of land ownership were changing. Small estates in far-flung corners of the country that had been acquired through marriage or inheritance were sold off by the larger landowners, either because they were impractical to administer efficiently or be-cause funds were needed to buy land that had come onto the market closer to home. But this process of consolidation varied

'I TOOK THEM . . . FOR A SORT OF HOUSES OR BARNS TO FODDER CATTLE IN.'

THE SO-CALLED 'AGRARIAN REVOLUTION' OF THE 18TH CENTURY LEFT

MANY SMALL-SCALE FARMERS UNTOUCHED.

considerably from region to region. In the home counties, for instance, new money moved out of London in an attempt to make the transition from merchant to landowning gentry, although land offered a safe investment, the returns it yielded throughout the eighteenth century were nowhere near as great as those from commerce, and upward social mobility and the desire for status played a part in most acquisitions by City parvenus. This tended to break up established patterns of ownership. Further afield, there was less competition and the great established families could control the market as they wished, buying or selling as the mood and the tides of fortune took them. This might mean swallowing up smaller estates, or it might not. In Cumbria in the late seventeenth and early eighteenth centuries, for example, the big landowners actually sold more land than they bought.

But the opportunities offered by agriculture certainly were growing. National and regional markets for produce began to take the place of local markets and subsistence farming as the demand for food grew with the population, which doubled during the eighteenth century. In the 1720s Daniel Defoe described how great droves of a thousand or two thousand geese and turkeys would be driven from Norfolk and Suffolk in August each year, the fowl feeding on harvest stubble in the fields as they went. Around 150,000 turkeys passed through to the London markets each season on a single route 'over Stratford-Bridge on the River Stour . . . and this one of the least passages'.

And what effect did all this activity have on the cottager? That is much harder to say. For those smallholders who produced enough to sell it was actually an opportunity rather than a threat. For labourers' real wages were rising for much of the eighteenth century, and their standard of living rose with them. Foreign visitors often found that rural housing conditions compared favourably with those of their European neighbours, a point made by the German pastor Carl Philipp Moritz during a tour of Kent in 1782:

> *An uncommon neatness in the structure of the houses . . . struck me with a pleasing surprise especially when I compare them with the long, rambling inconvenient and singularly mean cottages of our peasants.*

A YORKSHIRE COTTAGE. FOREIGN VISITORS OFTEN FOUND THAT RURAL HOUSING CONDITIONS COMPARED FAVOURABLY WITH THOSE AT HOME.

But, while it may have been overemphasized as a cause of changing rural housing patterns in the eighteenth century, there is no doubt that one phenomenon was responsible for the displacement of many cottagers, and the destruction of numbers of cottages – enclosure.

To speak in a determinate manner, we must establish some regular quantity intended to be brewed; and some certain size of the vessels. We will suppose the farmer has a copper, which, when filled to the top, holds a barrel, that is, six and thirty gallons; and we will say he is to brew five bushels of malt. He has this in the house, it has been ground a proper time, and there is nothing to be done but to put to it the water proper for its kind. Let the water be set on in the copper, and when it is pretty hot pour upon it half a peck of malt. This will keep in it spirit, soften it, and purify it, and make it heat regularly. When it begins to boil ladle it out into the mash vat, and there let it stand about a quarter of an hour.

It is often the necessity of the farmer to use but indifferent pond water in brewing. In this case let him pour half a peck of bran upon it instead of the malt, and when it boils scum that off. It will take the worst foulness of the water with it; and is to be given to the hogs. In the other case, when the water is tolerably pure, the malt is to be used, and is not to be scummed off, but to be ladled out with the water.

When it has stood about the time mentioned, the steam will be but little, and the farmer may look down into it and see his face in it. This is the country rule, for he cannot see it while the steam rises thick. Separate half a bushel of the malt, and let the rest run slowly and leisurely into the liquor when it is of this warmth; let it be well stirred about as it runs in, and thoroughly mixed when all is together.

It is a common practice to beat and stir up the malt in this first mash into a hasty pudding, but this is wrong. The whole brewing always succeeds better when it is only well mixed together without such beating. It receives the hot water the more freely, and gives strength to it in a fine manner. When the malt is thoroughly soaked, the hot water is to be ladled on by bowls full, and it is to be suffered to run out at the tap in a small stream, no thicker than a straw. In this manner, the liquor will run off clear, and will yet have the full strength and true flavour of the malt, according to its kind; and will much sooner be fine than in the common way . . .

When the first stirring of the malt is done, let the half bushel that was saved out be carefully spread over it; and then let some sacks, or other covering, be laid upon the tub to keep in the steam. The whole is to stand in this way about two hours and a half, and in that time the second copper of water is to be made boiling hot. This is to be poured on either briskly or slowly, according to the design of more or less small beer; and when it is in, let as much run off from the tap as will very near fill the copper. Put half a pound of fine sweet hops in a canvas bag, and throwing them into the copper boil them half an hour. Then take them out; and some fresh ones are then to be put in and to boil half an hour. The quantity of hops must be greater for beer, and less for ale.

If the beer be intended for keeping, half a pound of fresh hops should be put in every half hour, and the whole boiled briskly for an hour and an half. While this first copper of wort is boiling, some scalding hot water must be poured in upon the malt, bowl by bowl; and thus so much is to be got in and suffered to run off again, that there may be the quantity of another copper ready for boiling, by that time the first quantity is boiled off.

When this is drawn off the second running must be put in and boiled an hour, with nearly the same quantity of hops as at first; and while this is doing, preparation may be making for small beer, by pouring on such a quantity of water as the farmer chooses cold upon the grains all at once, or at twice. This must be boiled in the copper in the same manner as the ale wort, and must have the hops that were boiled before. Each copper of the small beer should be allowed an hour in boiling. In this manner five bushels of malt will make the farmer a hogshead of ale, and the same quantity of small beer; or if he chooses otherwise, his ale will be much the stronger and better . . . Let cleanliness be observed in every thing . . . Whoever intends to brew

at home, must look carefully himself into this article. Let a copper of water, or two if needful, be boiled several days before the brewing. Let the smaller utensils be boiled in it; and the larger be well scalded with it. Let them all be thoroughly cleaned after the scalding, and then scalded again. After this let them be exposed to the sun and air, so as to bleach and perfectly sweeten, but not so as to crack them; and after this let them be set by for use. If every thing be thus conducted, the malt suited to the intended kind of liquor, the water to the malt, and the quantity duly proportioned . . . and the vessels clean, there can be no doubt of the whole succeeding to credit and entire satisfaction.

FROM *A COMPLEAT BODY OF HUSBANDRY*, BY THOMAS HALE, 1758.

Roger Swillum's House

According to one writer in 1700, cottagers on the commons, 'having liv'd Time immemorial in such places', had 'as good a Title to their Habitation as if they had continu'd there from the Beginning of the World'. The 'right of commage', says Defoe, was something 'which the poor take to be as much their property, as a rich man's land is his own'. John Day kept two cows on the common at Highwood. But enclosure meant that

rights to such commons were often taken away from the cottager, along with the open field system. The ancient system of communally held land usually involved the land around a village being farmed in two or three large fields, with strips owned individually but crops and stock controlled cooperatively by the community. There were no physical boundaries to delineate ownership, and grazing rights to commons and waste were also held by villagers as of tradition.

The enclosing of open fields changed all this. It was a steady process, and far from exclusive to the eighteenth century – upwards of twenty per cent of land in England was enclosed during the seventeenth century, and a further eleven per cent between 1800 and 1914. Nevertheless, during the 1700s and either by private agreement or by Act of Parliament, fences, ditches and hedges were put in place, and the land became private property.

Enclosing by act required a two-thirds majority, not of land-holders, but by acreage. It followed that a single landowner could initiate the process, as Lord Craven did at Ashbury in Berkshire in 1770, and Lord Carbery at Laxton in Nottinghamshire two years later. Where several land-holders sought to enclose a parish, the process was as follows. First, those seeking change would meet to draw up a petition to submit to Parliament and decide on the commissioners who would carry out the process. When the act was awarded, an appointed surveyor would draw up plans of the area, and everybody claiming ownership or common rights would have to submit their claims to the commissioners – in writing. Once the commissioners had heard evidence of ownership from the various claimants, they decided on the value of each one's existing plot or plots and allotted new areas of land to them equal to the value of their previous holdings.

There were something like 5,250 Enclosure Acts passed by Parliament during the eighteenth and early nineteenth centuries. A further number, much harder to quantify, went through by private agreement. Although commissioners were by and large fair in their redistribution of land, the cottage-dweller with a small parcel of land and/or common rights was placed at a serious disadvantage, as the agricultural writer Arthur Young – a committed supporter of enclosure – was quick to point out:

What is it to the poor man to be told that the Houses of Parliament are extremely tender of property, while the father of the family is forced to sell his cow and his land because the one is not competent to the other; and being deprived of the only motive to industry, squanders the money, contracts bad habits, enlists for a soldier, and leaves the wife and children to the parish? . . . The poor in these parishes may say, and with truth, Parliament may be tender of property; all I know is, I had a cow, and act of Parliament has taken it from me.

In practice, the small owner-occupier who disagreed with enclosure was unlikely to be in a position to lodge an objection with the commissioners in writing. However, he or she might not even know of their impending fate – until 1774 it wasn't necessary to advertize an intention to seek a bill. Moreover, once enclosure had been agreed, the administrative costs of the process, the commissioners' fees and those of their surveyor, were met by levying a rate, which amounted to somewhere around £3 an acre. Subsequent costs, such as the erection of fences and hedges, could raise this as high as £12 an acre, a figure that was beyond the reach of many. Those cottagers who had common rights were allocated land to compensate them for their loss, but these plots were often too small to be economically viable, and large numbers were soon forced to sell up. In Buckinghamshire, for example, half of all landowners sold within two or three years of enclosure, a 150 per cent increase on the normal turnover per decade.

Perhaps most significantly of all, the removal of access to commons could radically change the rural worker's way of life. In the case of the poorest, the squatters who had built their cottages on common land, enclosure meant eviction and the demolition of their hovels. But others, too, had to face a change. Without the common, where would John Day gather the fuel for his fire, what was he to do with his two cows? And without the cows, what was he to do with his dairy and all its cheesemaking equipment? The traditional way of life, whereby the cottager could combine wage-labour or taskwork with small-scale food production, would disappear – as it often did – to be replaced by dependence on wages. Many labourers found themselves relying entirely on an employer for the first time in their lives. To some commentators, this was a good thing:

The benefit which [the poor] are supposed to reap from the commons . . . is an essential injury to them by being made a plea for their idleness . . . If you offer them work, they

*will tell you they must go to look up
their sheep, cut furzes, get their cow
out of the pound . . . The certain
weekly income of the husband's
labour, not attended by the anxiety of
the little farmer, will procure more
real comfort in his little cottage.*

However, it was becoming harder for
the labourer even to find a little cottage,
never mind procuring 'more real comfort'.
With enclosure, landlords could terminate existing agreements and impose
higher rents. While they had an incentive
to build farmhouses to exploit the pro-
ductivity of their new holdings, there was
little incentive to build labourers' housing.
It was quite the reverse in some areas,
where fears that cottagers would increase
the poor rate that landowners had to pay
led the latter deliberately to allow cottages
to deteriorate until they fell down. In
1775 Nathaniel Kent's *Hints of Gentlemen
of Landed Property* complained that

> *The shattered hovels which half the
> poor of this kingdom are obliged to
> put up with, is truly affecting to a
> heart fraught with humanity. Those
> who condescend to visit these miser-
> able tenements can testify that nei-
> ther health or decency can be pre-
> served in them.*

Kent's book contained plans for
model cottages. They are basic two-storey
affairs of brick or timber, built in pairs
with a living hall and pantry downstairs
and two bedchambers above. 'All that
is requisite,' he says, 'is a warm, comfortable, plain room for the poor inhabitants

'IF YOU OFFER THEM
WORK, THEY WILL TELL
YOU THEY MUST GO TO
LOOK UP THEIR SHEEP,
CUT FURZES, GET THEIR
COW OUT OF THE
POUND', IT WAS
ARGUED OF 'WORKSHY'
COTTAGERS.

DOMESTIC BLISS, PAINTING BY GEORGE MORLAND DEPICTING A CON-
TENTED FAMILY OF COTTAGERS; THE REALITY WAS MUCH DIFFERENT.

to eat their morsel in, an oven to bake their bread, a little receptacle for their small beer and provisions and two wholesome apartments, one for the man and his wife and another for his children.' Hardly a palace, but still beyond the reach of large numbers of Georgian rural labourers.

For some cottagers, though, the renewed interest that major landowners were taking in their estates in the eighteenth century led not to eviction and homelessness, but actually to an improvement in their housing conditions. At the beginning of the century a country house and its garden stood like an oasis of order in the countryside. Within a walled enclosure, walks, canals and trees encircled the house in strictly regimented lines and formal geometrical patterns, the epitome of nature tamed and regulated. Perhaps an avenue of limes or elms, aligned on the main axis of the house, stretched out into the distance to assert a landowner's dominance and power over his estates. But the area beyond, including any village or other small settlement, was of no concern to him.

The famous series of bird's-eye views of country houses published by Leonard Knyff and Johannes Kip in the early 1700s illustrate these boundaries perfectly. In engraving after engraving, little cottages sprawl indiscriminately in groups of twos and threes on the edge of the picture, or line up along the meandering lanes that flank a gentleman's estate, a foil to the formal vistas and geometrical parterres.

But with the introduction from France in the early eighteenth century of the ha-ha, a sunken fence that could keep stock away from the immediate vicinity of the house while maintaining an uninterrupted view over the surrounding area, the garden walls came down. Huge landscape parks swallowed up villages and hamlets; lakes and temples took the place of cottages; whole communities were displaced and – if they were lucky – rehoused out of sight.

The most famous instance of a community being uprooted wholesale and set down again in a purpose-built village is Nuneham Courtenay in Oxfordshire. In 1756 the first Lord Harcourt commissioned the architect Stiff Leadbetter to build him a new Palladian villa at Nuneham, a cross between a family seat and a country retreat. The site was chosen to make full use of views across to the spires of Oxford, and since the existing village was rather in the way, Harcourt decided to demolish it. A new church in the form of a classical temple was put up in the park, and the village was rebuilt out of sight of the

AN ILLUSTRATION FROM *THE DESERTED VILLAGE*, BY FRANCIS WHEATLEY.

house along the London road. It took the form of two parallel rows of cottages of brick and timber, single-storeyed with two rooms and projecting dormers lighting two further rooms in the roofspace. The result was described in 1788 by the Rev. Stebbing Shaw, who writes that the twenty or so houses 'are divided into two separate dwellings so that forty families may here, by the liberal assistance of his lordship, enjoy the comforts of industry under a wholesome roof who otherwise might have been doomed to linger out their days in the filthy hut of poverty'.

Not everyone agreed with Shaw. One of the reasons for Nuneham's fame is that it served as the model for 'Sweet Auburn' in Oliver Goldsmith's classic eighteenth-century elegy on rural depopulation, *The Deserted Village*:

> *A time there was, ere England's griefs began,*
> *When every rood of ground maintained its man;*
> *For him light labour spread her wholesome store,*
> > *Just gave what life required, but gave no more . . .*
> > *But times are altered; trade's unfeeling train*
> > *Usurp the land and dispossess the swain;*
> > *Along the lawn, where scattered hamlets rose,*
> > *Unwieldy wealth and cumbrous pomp repose!*

'AND ALL THE VILLAGE TRAIN, FROM LABOUR FREE,/LED UP THEIR SPORTS BENEATH THE SPREADING TREE/ WHILE MANY A PASTIME CIRCLED IN THE SHADE,/THE YOUNG CONTENDING AS THE OLD SURVEYED.'
THE DESERTED VILLAGE

For Goldsmith, 'The man of wealth and pride/Takes up a space that many poor supplied', as his great landscape park, 'where solitary sports are seen,/Indignant spurns the cottage from the green'.

This is a little hard, perhaps. Stebbing Shaw's assessment of Harcourt's new village as a welcome alternative to 'the filthy hut of poverty' is no doubt closer to the truth (contemporary rumours that he had built a grotto in his grounds from the bones of his villagers were untrue). Goldsmith's poem is of more significance as an early expression of the Romantic sensibility that would idealize the cottage and rural life in general over the next century, and that would also criticize Harcourt – not for his apparent lack of reverence for tradition, but for his taste in producing over-formal and serried ranks of cottages rather than picturesque and varied groupings.

But Nuneham Courtenay was only one of a number of purpose-built villages created in the eighteenth century as a result of the whims and changing tastes of landowners. There was Milton Abbas in Dorset, for example, built in the 1770s and 1780s by William Chambers and Capability Brown for the Earl of Dorchester. A group of forty Dorset cob-and-thatch cottages, complete with their own church, replaced an earlier village that stood too close to the walls of Dorchester's Milton Abbey. Lowther in Westmorland (1765-73) was an ambitious scheme by Sir James Lowther and the Adam brothers to provide a miniature 'city' for industrial workers, complete with a circus and two squares. Never completed, its 'fantastic incongruity' was commented on by one tourist in 1802: 'These groups of houses were built for the labourers of Lord Lowther but from their desolate deserted appearance it should seem that no sufficient encouragement has been held out to their inhabitants to continue in them.' Such experiments in social engineering were rare, however, and for most of the eighteenth century traditional rural worker-housing followed much the same pattern as it had in the previous century. One,

ONE OF 40 ESTATE COT-
TAGES BUILT AT MILTON
ABBAS, DORSET, BY
WILLIAM CHAMBERS AND
CAPABILITY BROWN.

COTTAGE ON THE ESTATE OF
NEW HOUGHTON, NORFOLK,
BUILT *c.* 1729.

two, three or four rooms were common, local materials were used, and the same patterns of ownership remained, with cottages being put up by landowners, by tenant farmers, by speculative builders and by country labourers themselves. Not all such buildings were squalid slums, by any means, but as the century drew to a close there was growing disquiet about the conditions in which some of the poorer members of rural society were forced to live.

A chance conversation with 'several gentlemen of landed property . . . on the ruinous state of the cottages of this kingdom' led the Bath architect John Wood the younger to see for himself the living conditions of the English labourer. With an unusual sensitivity to the needs of working people and a commendably practical approach to the business of architecture – 'no architect can form a convenient plan, unless he ideally places himself in the situation of the person for whom he designs' – he resolved to visit cottagers, to ask them what they wanted from a house, 'to feel as the cottager himself'.

What Wood saw in his travels may not have surprised him, but it certainly distressed him:

> *Shattered, dirty, inconvenient, miserable hovels, scarcely affording a shelter*
> *for beasts of the forest; much less were they proper habitations for the human*
> *species; nay it is impossible to describe the miserable condition of the poor cot-*
> *tager, of which I was too often the melancholy spectator.*

Even the better kind of cottages were wet and damp, partly because of their situation, but

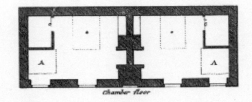

Chamber floor

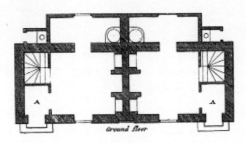

Ground floor

Although I cannot recommend timber buildings, knowing them to be attended with many and great inconveniencies, particularly their being hot in summer and cold in winter; their being too liable to fire, and their being continually in want of repairs; yet as some Gentlemen may be desirous of following the practice, I will give them the best advice I can, and this is no way better to be done, than by showing the method of framing the front and end of the double cottage. The scantling of the timber necessary for cottages of this sort is but small, the strength of the building depending more on the mechanical construction, than on the size and quantity of the materials.

All timber buildings must be supported on a brick or stone foundation of about two feet high above the natural ground, on this foundation must be laid the sill, AA in [*fig.* 1, opposite page] which represents the framing of the south side of tages; into the sill must b posts BB, and all the other sill must be six inches bro thick, and as it will be dif procure timber long enou for the sill to be of one piece, let it be scarfed or lengthened with a dove-

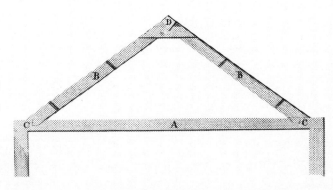

tailed joint; the studs that form the jambs of the doors and windows are to to be six inches broad and four thick, all the others only two inches thick; the braces to be also six inches square.

The girder CC is to be tenoned at each end, into the upright posts with a dove-tailed tenon; and scarfed with an indented joint. This girder to be six inches square, and its office is to support the floor of the chambers; the studs in the lower tier are tenoned both into the sill, and into the under side of the girder; the other studs only into the sill, as cutting so many mortices in the girder would weaken it too much. But to supply the place of a mortice, let there, between every two studs, be tightly driven a piece of inch board and nailed to the under side of the girder, as expressed by the dotted line, the same must be done both on the upper and lower sides of the braces as mortices to the studs, that rest on those pieces. The office of the braces is not only to keep the framing steady, and l to end, but also to admit hs to be made use of; and l be] leaning towards the e work, and not be guilty frequent error of placing m the contrary way, as I have shown by the dotted lines xx in the upper tier [*fig.* 1, this page].

The wall plate DD, which in these buildings is more properly the architrave, to be four inches thick, scarfed as the girder, and dove-tailed its whole depth into the heads of the angular posts. The studs in the second tier are to be tenoned both into the girder and into the architrave, but the others only into the girder, and secured at top as those in the lower tier. The second figure [at right] represents the framing of the ends, and needs no further explanation, than that the timbers AA, and BB, are to be tenoned into the angular posts with a dove-tailed tenon, and the timber CC, tenoned into the same posts with a common tenon. This piece may be placed either higher or lower, at the discretion of the builder, as its use is chiefly to give an opportunity of using short stuff.

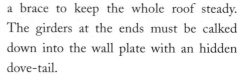

The roofs of these buildings differ from those of stone or brick buildings, as their office is as much to keep the oposite sides of the building together, as to cover the cottages, and must therefore be framed with principal rafters, as *fig.* 8 [opposite page], where A is the girder, or span beam; BB, the principal rafters. Both girder and rafters are six inches by four; the rafters to be abutted into the girder as at C, and halved together at the point. Care must be taken that the toe of the rafter be within the upright of the inside of the framing. Into these rafters must be framed purlines of six by two, and at the point, between each pair of principals, must be a ridge piece of quarter four inches square, as at D, the upper sides of which must bevel with the rafter, but the under sides square the one to the other. These ridge pieces must be supported by a small collar oo; on these

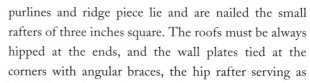

Fig. 8

purlines and ridge piece lie and are nailed the small rafters of three inches square. The roofs must be always hipped at the ends, and the wall plates tied at the corners with angular braces, the hip rafter serving as a brace to keep the whole roof steady. The girders at the ends must be calked down into the wall plate with an hidden dove-tail.

The floors will differ from that in [*fig.* 8, this page], in nothing but that the ends of the joists must be calked down to the girder, as the girders of the roof are calked down to the wall plate. And lest the ends of the joists should rise, it will be necessary to fasten them with a large staple drove over them into the girders. But great care must be taken not to let the staple pass through the joist into the girder, as that would entirely destroy the operation of the dove-tail, whose office is manifestly to keep the sides of the building from spreading, both by these joists of the floor, and by the girders of the roof; from hence will appear the reason of scarfing the architrave and girder with an indented joint, because that method of scarfing resists the pull or thrust both lengthways and breadthways, whereas a dove-tail scarf, as in the sill, resists only the pull lengthways.

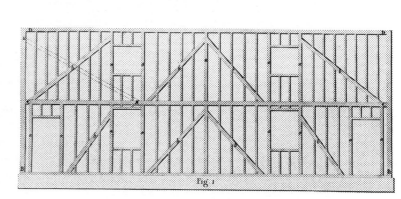

Fig. 1

FROM *A SERIES OF PLANS FOR COTTAGES OR HABITATIONS OF THE LABOURER,* BY JOHN WOOD, 1781

also because of the habit of having floors sunk below ground level. At six inches of free-stone or nine of brick, their external walls were too thin. 'In the winter, I have seen the inside of these walls covered with ice from the roof to the foundation', Wood remarks. They had no privies at all. And where there was a second storey, the stairs, which usually went up the side of the chimney, were too steep, and it was common for a family to sleep together in the unpartitioned roof space, which was stifling hot in summer and freezing cold in winter. Commenting on the indecency of one chamber for a large family, Wood says that:

> *It is melancholy to see a man and his wife, and sometimes half a dozen children crowded together in the same room, nay often in the same bed; the horror is still heightened, and the inconveniency increased at the time when the woman is in child-bed, or in case of illness, or of death . . .*

CONDITIONS INSIDE THE COTTAGE WERE OFTEN CRAMPED AND SQUALID –

FAMILIES SPENT AS MUCH TIME AS POSSIBLE IN THE OPEN AIR.

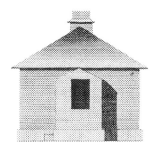

The fruits of Wood's research were published in 1781 as *A Series of Plans for Cottages or Habitations of the Labourer*, the first book to be devoted entirely to the subject of cottages.

DESIGNS FROM JOHN WOOD'S *SERIES OF PLANS FOR COTTAGES . . .*, 1781.

Wood begins by setting out seven principles of building. Any cottage must be dry and healthy: set on an open site with a fall away from the building, with rooms no less than eight feet high and floors at least sixteen inches above the ground. It must also be warm, cheerful and comfortable, with walls of a reasonable thickness (sixteen inches if the cottage is built of stone, or a brick and a half if of brick), a screened entrance and an east or south facing aspect. 'So like the feelings of men in an higher sphere are those of the poor cottager, that if his habitation be warm, cheerful and comfortable, he will return to it with gladness, and abide in it with pleasure.'

Wood's third principle concerns what he calls convenience. There must be a porch to hold the labourer's tools, a shed as a pantry and a fuel store, a privy (which will serve as 'an introduction to cleanliness'), and where there is an upper storey, stairs not less than three feet wide. Parents, daughters and sons should all have separate bedrooms. This contrasts with Nathaniel Kent's belief that separate accommodation for boys and girls is an unnecessary extravagance, since 'the boys find employment in farmhouses at an early age'.

But Wood is not unmindful of the expense of building. His fourth principle is that no cottage should be more than twelve feet wide, since any greater span would require longer, stronger and more costly timbers for the roof and floor. In any case, 'twelve feet is sufficient for a dwelling that is to be deemed a cottage; if it be wider, it approaches too near to what I would call a house for a superior tradesman'.

Fifthly, Wood proposes that cottages should always be built in pairs, so that the occupants can come to each other's aid in case of sickness or accident. Sixthly, they should be built of the best possible materials, so that they will stand longer and keep their appearance. 'I would by no means have these cottages fine, yet I recommend regularity, which is beauty; regularity will render them ornaments to the country, instead of their being as at present disagreeable objects.' And lastly, he holds that a piece of ground for a garden should be allotted to every cottage, and that there should be a spring or at least a well nearby.

There are several intriguing features about Wood's *Series of Plans for Cottages*, not least his compassion for the labouring classes. At one point he criticizes a Dorset landowner for the poor standard of a row of four new farmworkers' cottages that are already falling down. They have a single chamber for the whole family up in the triangular roof-space, no screened entrances and, 'what adds to the shamelessness of it', only thin unjointed boards as partitions between each house:

It is a pity that gentlemen, who build cottages for the accommodation of their labourers, do not study . . . conveniency and decency for the sake of the inhabitants; for, believe me, the poor man wishes for conveniency, but knows not how to remedy himself; and would be decent, was it in his power.

Another point is that Wood is a practising architect – the leading architect in Bath during the second half of the eighteenth century, in fact – and one of the great Palladians of his age. That the creator of the Royal Crescent and the Bath Assembly Rooms should concern himself with the design of labourers' cottages marks a departure from the established practice of leaving such projects to the master-builders and mason-contractors who would carry out the actual work. (Although Wood was not the first prominent architect to engage in the building of worker-housing; John Carr of York had a hand in Harewood village in Yorkshire in the 1760s and 1770s, while working on a new house for Edwin Lascelles, Lord Harewood). Wood's book is more than the type of self-advertisement that was usual for the period. Full of costings and construction details, it is much more of a handbook for landowners with little knowledge of building to peruse and then to hand over to local craftsmen.

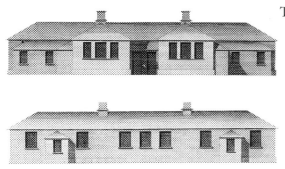

The forty-five plans that make up the bulk of the book range in size and extent from the simple one-room house, twelve feet square and seven feet, six inches from floor to the top of the wallplate, to two-, three- and four-room cottages. In each case the cottage consists of a living room with beds occupying the other main chambers. Most bedrooms have fireplaces. In addition, there is usually a pantry, sometimes a wash-house and invariably an outside privy, behind the main block and often back-to-back with the entrance porch.

Within this apparently straightforward scheme Wood comes up with a surprising variety of permutations. Several of his plans for two-room cottages, for instance, are single-storeyed and detached, with either projecting porches or vestibules. Another is also detached, but two-storeyed, with a staircase placed behind the house:

This cottage will suit only an artificer, with a wife, or a wife and small child, who can afford to give a little more rent than the inhabitants of the preceding cottages, such as masons, bricklayers, thatchers, plaisterers, and many others who earn fifteen to twenty shillings per week; it will also suit many artificers in several manufactories, who are obliged to do their work at home.

And by resiting the chimney and the door, 'a bed may be very conveniently placed in the lower room, which will render this cottage commodious to a much larger family'.

Other two-roomed houses are built in pairs, or in terraces of four. These last are 'proper for large towns or cities', says the architect; but prospective landlords should 'by

COTTAGES AT HAREWOOD VILLAGE IN YORKSHIRE, DESIGNED BY JOHN
CARR OF YORK, 1760. AT THE SAME TIME, CARR WAS ALSO BUILDING A
HOUSE FOR LORD HAREWOOD TKTKTK TKTKTK ADRIAN!

all means avoid letting the stairs begin to rise from the porch so as to make room for a bed below, in order to prevent any avaricious inhabitant taking an inmate'.

The simplicity of the cottages depicted in *A Series of Plans* makes them a delight to look at, even today. Although by modern standards they would have been terribly cramped, their stark, clean lines and severe simplicity and the evidence they show of Wood's concern for convenience and decency mark a great leap forward in the design of the English cottage.

Yet almost as soon as Wood's book appeared it was out of date, not because housing standards for the lower classes had overtaken his plans, but because those clean lines and that severe simplicity, the 'regularity' that he and his generation prized so highly in architecture, were going out of fashion. As the eighteenth century drew to a close, the peasant in his irregular tumble-down hovel was being elevated to the status of art-object, another interesting feature to take its place among the grottos and temples that peppered the landscape. And even more extraordinarily, the landed classes were about to begin cottage-building in earnest, not for their tenantry, but for themselves.

CHAPTER IV

A Cottage of Gentility

1790-1840

He pass'd a cottage with a double coach-house,
A cottage of gentility!
And he own'd with a grin
That his favourite sin
Is pride that apes humility.

ROBERT SOUTHEY, 'THE DEVIL'S WALK', 1799

Something strange happened to the cottage at the end of the eighteenth century. In 1781 Wood the younger's utilitarian *A Series of Plans for Cottages or Habitations of the Labourer* had appealed to a landowner's sense of social responsibility, to his or her duty to improve the often appalling living conditions of his tenants. A mere thirty years later Robert Ferrars, in *Sense and Sensibility*, declared: 'I am exceedingly fond of a cottage. There is always so much comfort, so much elegance about them. And I protest, if I had any money to spare I should buy a little land and build one myself.' Comfort? Elegance? Jane Austen and John Wood clearly had very different ideas about what constituted a cottage.

So what had happened to the genre in the intervening three decades? The answer is inextricably bound up with much broader cultural trends – the idea of the Picturesque and its richer relation, the Romantic Movement.

By the later eighteenth century, the early Georgian demand for rigid canons of taste that had led to the dominance of neo-classicism, with its emphasis on the application of rules and order in all branches of the arts, was coming under fire. Edmund Burke, in his *Philosophical Enquiry into the Origins of our Ideas of the Sublime and the Beautiful* (1756), was one of the first major commentators to point out that, attractive though symmetry and regularity may be, there were other types of scenes, other categories of art and architecture which, while not conforming to classical convention, might be equally appealing. Cataracts and mountains, for example, were vast and irregular, frightening even, and yet they could still be attractive, producing an emotional response which was wholly at odds with the essentially intellectual nature of classicism.

The idea that it was permissible for a man of taste to admire Nature – a notion which would have been completely incomprehensible to earlier generations – soon took root, as other aesthetic theorists developed Burke's ideas. To his two aesthetic categories – the Sublime, which was dark, gloomy and vast, and the Beautiful, which was smooth and polished – was added a third category, the Picturesque. The Picturesque was defined in 1798 by its chief proponent, William Gilpin, as 'that kind of beauty which would look well in a picture'. Gilpin meant by this the sort of ideal landscape that adhered to the pattern set out in Claude's visions of the Roman campagna – foreground figures, architectural features in the middle distance, hazy blue hills in the background and the whole scene framed by overhanging trees and verdure. Describing objects that produced the Picturesque effect, Gilpin cited their roughness, variety, accident, contrast and ruggedness.

Such a sophisticated legitimization of unsophisticated natural scenery was, of course, underpinned by the Romantics' emphasis on Nature as a positive spiritual force. They knew their Rousseau, with his talk of 'noble savages' and his assertion that civilization was a fall from Nature, a backward step. They had read the 1755 English edition of the Abbé Laugier's *Essay on Architecture*, with its call for architecture to return to the clarity and directness of the primitive hut erected by the First Man. 'It is by coming near the simplicity of this first model', claimed Laugier, 'that we lay hold on true perfection.' And for Wordsworth, Coleridge and their contemporaries, the implication was clear – the

BY THE LATER 18TH CENTURY A THIRD AESTHETIC CATEGORY WAS ADDED

TO THOSE OF THE SUBLIME AND THE BEAUTIFUL – THE PICTURESQUE.

countryside was good, pure, uncorrupted, while the town was bad. Coleridge saw the 'eternal language' of God in lakes and shores and mountain crags, while Wordsworth recalled with joy how as a child he had 'bounded o'er the mountains, by the sides/Of the deep rivers, and the lonely streams,/Wherever nature led.' And as the nineteenth century began, nature led straight to an idealized vision of rural life.

It was a short step from that vision to a new appreciation of the cottage as both a scenic device and an exemplar of a more innocent, prelapsarian way of life. Uvedale Price, who with Richard Payne Knight was the ablest and most convincing of the mid-Georgian Picturesque theorists, extolled the visual potential of rural worker-housing, writing that 'The characteristic beauties of a village are intricacy, variety and play of outline . . . The houses should therefore . . . differ as much in their disposition from those of a regularly built city, as the trees, which are meant to have the character of natural groups, should differ from those of an avenue.' Instead of sweeping a village away out of sight, as George Vernon had done at Sudbury in the 1660s, or creating neat, uniform rows of labourers' dwellings parading up to the gates of a country house, as the first Earl Harcourt had done at Nuneham Courtenay a century later, a landowner could use cottages to create a Picturesque landscape. But while the Romantic poets might rhapsodize over the moral virtues of life in a farm labourer's one-room cottage, those who were better acquainted with the scenic potential of such a building quickly realized that a little help would be needed. So in 1806 Richard Colt Hoare converted a small thatched keeper's cottage on the edge of the gardens at Stourhead in Wiltshire into an ornamental feature, adding a Gothic seat and porch. Nestled among the temples and grottoes put up by his grandfather, Stourhead's Gothic Cottage is a perfect example of the change in taste that turned

THE GOTHIC COTTAGE AT STOURHEAD IN WILTSHIRE, A PICTURESQUE CONCEIT.

rural worker-housing from an object of contempt into a work of art. That art achieved perhaps its highest form in the early 1800s on a corner of the Blaise Castle estate at Henbury, a few miles north of Bristol.

Blaise had been bought in 1789 by a Quaker banker, John Scandrett Harford. Harford wanted a new house and landscaped grounds. His architect, William Paty, duly provided the former in 1795-96 – a rather sober, unadorned Georgian block – while Humphry Repton came up with the latter at about the same time. Fifteen years later Harford conceived the notion of creating a small settlement of cottages for his retired estate workers, and called in John Nash, who had designed a conservatory for Blaise in 1806.

The result was Blaise Hamlet, an impossibly quaint group of ten cottages on 1¾ acres ranged irregularly round a 'village green'. Variously described as 'on the verge of noddyland' and 'responsible for some of the worst sentimentalities of England', the

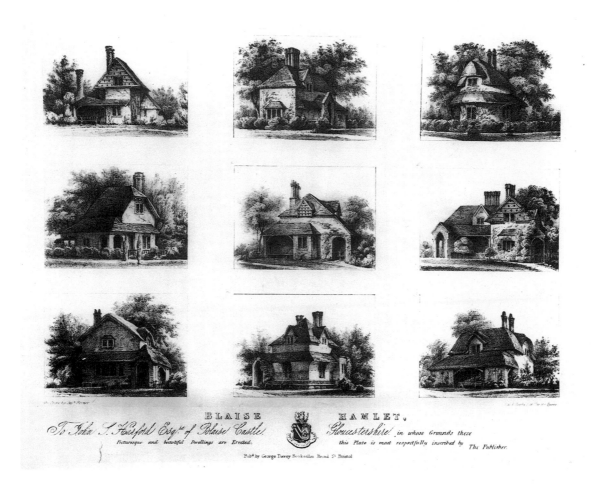

BLAISE HAMLET,
To John S. Harford Esqre of Blaise Castle.
Picturesque and beautiful Dwellings are Erected.
Gloucestershire, in whose Grounds these
this Plate is most respectfully inscribed by The Publisher.
Publd by George Davey Bookseller Broad St Bristol

BLAISE HAMLET, DESIGNED AS HOUSING FOR RETIRED ESTATE WORKERS BY
JOHN NASH FOR JOHN SCANDRETT HARFORD AT HENBURY NEAR BRISTOL.

Hamlet is nevertheless a tour de force of Picturesque theory and the Romantic idealization of country living. Nash ensured that roughness, accident, variety and contrast were in abundance: no two houses are the same, though all are walled with irregularly set rough stone. Tall chimneys of moulded brick in different patterns tower above layer upon layer of deeply overhanging thatch and tile of different shapes and sizes. There are crown various plan-forms, from Circular Cottage, named for its semi-circular bay, to Diamond Cottage, a square plan set at forty-five degrees to the village green. Oak Cottage was given a trunk-flanked porch between cruciform windows, and stone benches were thoughtfully provided for Harford's aged (and presumably Picturesque) pensioners. When it was built Blaise Hamlet was surrounded by trees, which must have added to the fairytale atmosphere, as if one had suddenly come upon a whole village of Hansel and Gretel cottages.

Internally the cottages were quite simple, consisting of sitting room, kitchen and

NASH ENSURED THAT AT BLAISE HAMLET THERE WAS ROUGHNESS, VARIETY
AND CONTRAST IN ABUNDANCE. NO TWO HOUSES ARE THE SAME.

pantry on the ground floor, with chambers above. Facilities were adequate, if hardly lux-
urious: each house had a privy, and coppers and ovens were provided, although an
unsigned note among the estate papers stipulates that 'the gardener must . . . find out the
smallest sized coppers and ovens that will be sufficient for the sort of people who are to
live in the Cottages'. Harford seems to have become quite anxious about the cost of his
new village, writing on 18 August 1810 that plans to build on pantries, rather than simply incorporating them in the main body of each cottage, would 'very much lengthen out

the Building and enhance the expence'. But from the outset, visual effect was to take precedence over price. Nash's assistant replied, 'If we make them *all* so it will very much injure (if not entirely destroy) the picturesque effect of the Cottages where so much depends upon the leantoos and Sheds etc to make a variety in their form.'

Sometime in the early 1820s a set of lithographs of the Hamlet appeared, with a lyrical introduction:

> *The Air of Comfort diffused over these little Dwellings; the play of Light and Shadow produced by their Projections and Recesses, which afford shelter to a variety of Creepers; the highly Ornamental and varied Character of the Chimnies; and the Beauty of the surrounding little Gardens, glittering throughout the Summer with Flowers of the brightest hues, and guarded from the intruding hand by Hedges of Sweet-Briar, suggest the most pleasing Images to the Fancy, and shed a romantic and poetical Character over this favoured Asylum.*

An asylum indeed, for there is something faintly unhinged about the determined quaintness of Blaise. And yet it works. In Nash's hands, the cottage had indeed been elevated into an art form.

꿍 꿍 꿍

Blaise Hamlet was always intended as a sort of glorified rest home for retired estate workers, and John Harford no doubt agreed with John Claudius Loudon's remarks on *Forming, Improving and Managing Country Residences* (1806): 'The wants of man in the lowest stage of society are comparatively few . . . when he is no longer capable of toil, he retires under the shelter of his cottage, and leaves the world as obscurely as he came into it.' But as landed society came to realize the attraction of the cottage as a Picturesque object, it also saw the potential for developing the form into something to meet the needs of the gentry – a rural retreat which 'affords the necessary conveniences for persons of refined manners and habits', as one early-nineteenth-century writer put it.

The result was a reinterpretation of the whole idea of the cottage. James Malton, whose *Essay on British Cottage Architecture* (1798) helped to pioneer the cottage ornée, as such larger variations on the vernacular theme became known, went right to the heart of the issue. Citing Dr Johnson's definition of the cottage as 'a mean habitation', he says:

> *With deference to such high authorities, I have led myself to conceive very differently of a Cottage; which may, I think, as well be the habitation of a substantial farmer or affluent gentleman, as the dwelling of the hedger and ditcher – 'a mean habitation', in the country or elsewhere, I would call a mean habitation.*

Malton's image of the cottage is a small house in the country, of odd, irregular form, with

DESIGNS FOR 'PEASANTS' HUTS FROM JAMES MALTON'S *ESSAY ON BRITISH COTTAGE ARCHITECTURE*, 1798.

I will here take occasion to remark on the many instances of incongruity that are daily committed by those who erect what they pleased to call Cottages, as to the formation of the windows. The most general form of Cottage windows are three: and these are simply either a rectangular opening or compounded of two, three, or more such openings; or the opening being lofty, is divided into two heights, where

the top lights are less in height than the lower; or where both top and bottom divisions are equal.

These are all the variety I remember to have obvserved in the simple British Cottage, of which numerous instances may be seen by all who have inquiring eyes and take the natural not the affected Cottage for their guide. It is however very common to find, of the latter description, the affected Cottage, together with the strictest attention to uniformity in the outward construction of the building, that the windows will be fashioned after the mode of castle or convent windows, which are as unlike those appropriate to Cottages as are Venetian; both the fashion and construction of such being far from simple and beyond the capacity or intention of the rustic architect to execute. Others however will go still farther, and construct windows with compound arches or enriched with the circular ramifications of Gothic tracery, all of which I have seen executed, and have heard called Cottage windows; than which no forms could well be more foreign.

Various are the designs which may be given for the tracery, or small bars, of Cottage windows. The most general figures are oblong squares, lozenges, mixed hexagons, or hexagons and lozenges mixed . . . each of the latter designs being all composed of right lines, setting aside the beauty of their forms, are the most proper for such glazings.

The aptitude of windows of such construction to the Cottage fabric is of universal acquiescence; nevertheless well-founded objections are urged against Cottage windows in general, as rendering rooms very cold in winter by admission of too much air; and that they are much subject to destruction from high winds, unless well stiffened by small iron bars. All which is very true; but might, I think, easily be obviated, were the whole framework made of the materials of the

patent fan-light sashes, which could readily be worked of any pattern desired . . . having a rabbet on each side the center rise, the glass could be neatly fitted in, and fixed with putty, and thereby be made perfectly air tight; while the bars themselves need not be broader, but rather narrower than the usual breadth of leaden divisions; at the same time, the uniform neatness of the whole, by excluding the necessity of iron bars, and having a small projecting bead on the inner face, would add considerably to the acknowledged beauty of casement windows.

The expense in the first instance would certainly be augmented; but the durability of the materials would preclude all after costs, which unavoidably occur in the usual mode of glazing with leaden divisions, independant of other weighty objections. It is not proposed nor expected, that this mode of glazing should become general, or extend to the peasant's hut; but it could be well applied to the gentleman's retreat, or used by the farmer mindful of domestic comfort.

Throughout the entire of these

designs, I have constantly aimed at throwing the light into the apartments by openings in the middle of the side or end of the room; and this from one large window, in preference to two with a pier between them, which, no matter how small, always makes an apartment heavy, and gives a dull rebuff at entrance, extremely unpleasant. This effect is strongly experienced in the smaller class of town dwellings, particularly when the pier is from six to eight feet wide.

Though I cannot agree with the author of a late publication, who, speaking of rural structures in general, observes that, 'so much is irregularity of parts a constituent of beauty, that regularity may almost be said to be deformity'; yet do I most decidedly admit that a well chosen irregularity is most pleasing; but it does not of consequence follow that all irregularity must necessarily be picturesque. To combine irregularity into pic turesque is the excellence of Cottage construction.

FROM JAMES MALTON, *ESSAY ON BRITISH COTTAGE ARCHITECTURE*, 1798.

what he describes as 'a contented, chearful, inviting aspect':

> *There are many indescribable somethings that must necessarily combine to
> give to a dwelling this distinguishing character. A porch at entrance; irregu-
> lar breaks in the direction of the walls; one part higher than another; various
> roofing of different materials, thatch particularly, boldly projecting; fronts
> partly built of walls of brick, partly weather boarded, and partly brick-
> noggin dashed; casement window lights, are all conducive, and constitute its
> features.*

By defining the cottage in such purely visual terms, Malton acknowledges his debt
to the Picturesque Movement. He goes on to quote from Payne Knight's *The Landscape*,
which contains in Malton's view the best description of a cottage he has met with:

> *Its roof, with reeds and mosses cover'd o'er,*
> *And honey-suckles climbing round the door,*
> *While mantling vines along its walls are spread,*
> *And clust'ring ivy decks the chimney's head!*

Ironically, Payne Knight was quick to condemn the fashion for 'primitive' architecture,
describing rustic lodges, dressed cottages and pastoral seats as having a strong character
of affectation, 'the rusticity of the first being that of a clown in a pantomime, and the simplicity of the others that of a shepherdess in a French opera'.

The fourteen designs appended to Malton's *Essay* herald just how all-embracing the
term 'cottage' was to become, cutting right across the social spectrum by the early years of
the nineteenth century. Beginning at the bottom end of the scale, he submits 'to the notice
of those gentlemen and farmers, who construct such dwellings for their labourers', four
sets of plans and elevations for 'peasants' huts'. The main body of each cottage is two-
storeyed, fifteen by eleven feet, and consists of a living room with a bedchamber over, and
a single-storey lean-to that contains a 'useful small room for grown children, or a place for
a sick bed' and a space for a scullery, piggery 'or aught else that may be thought most
advisable'. But this is not the simply utilitarian housing that the Georgian rural worker so
desperately needed. These peasants' huts are features in a landscape, coming straight out
of a painting by Gainsborough or Morland and exhibiting all the qualities of diversity and
irregularity that proponents of the Picturesque prized so highly. While thatch, lattice windows and half-doors (through which a contented peasantry idles away its days gossiping
to neighbours) are common to all, the façades are weather-boarded or timber-framed,
infilled with plaster or brick. Oriels break through here, two-storey bays there, and one
upper storey is jettied out over rustic columns.

This adoption of rustic elements and materials is also carried through into Malton's
larger designs. A house 'calculated both in appearance and conveniences for the accommodation of a genteel family' contains withdrawing room, breakfast parlour, dining room

SCENES FROM A BUCKINGHAMSHIRE COTTAGE, SHOW 'A CONTENTED,

CHEERFUL, INVITING ASPECT'.

and kitchen on the ground floor, with four bedrooms above – a substantial house, with its entrance recessed between projecting wings. Yet what Malton perceives as the elements of the traditional cottage are ruthlessly applied to the exterior of the larger house as well. The thatch is there, the lattices, the rustic columns, the mixture of weather-boarding and stucco. Even when more formal features are introduced – a 'habitation [that] has more the air of the residence of the retired gentleman', displays this riot of vernacular elements, a very unvernacular pedimented porch with coupled columns – the same determination is there to conjure up a painterly and wholly fictional association with rural life: the columns are 'roughly carved in imitation of the bark of a tree, and painted so as to resemble it'.

Other writers were quick to see the potential of the cottage ornée. The gentrified cottage showed the same concern with the massing of varied elements, the same use of 'rustic' features such as thatch and rough walling, as its smaller cousin. The main difference was that it was intended for a different class of occupant, and so was quite naturally bigger – much bigger in some cases, with perhaps eight or ten rooms or more. Throughout the first decades of the nineteenth century architects flooded the market with pattern books for cottages both large and small, with titles such as *Designs for Cottages, Cottage Farms and other Rural Buildings* (J. M. Gandy, 1805), *Designs for Elegant Cottages and Small Villas* (E. Gyfford, 1806), or *Rural Residences, consisting of a series of Designs for Cottages, Decorated Cottages, Small Villas and other Ornamental Buildings* (J. Papworth, 1818). The buildings they portray seem, like Nash's Blaise Hamlet, at once both charming and faintly ridiculous.

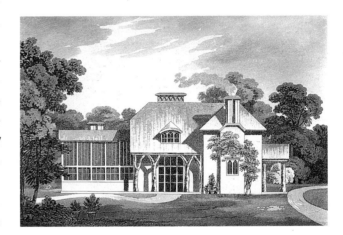

Diamond-paned dormers break through steeply pitched thatch; wooden columns, carved and painted to resemble bark, support verandas and porches; and everywhere there is a determined asymmetry, a self-conscious and very artificial desire to avoid the artificiality of balanced and integrated elements. But the style was wonderfully adaptable to different requirements, from labourers' houses and gate lodges to senior estate workers' houses and country retreats for gentlemen.

A single example can serve to illustrate the whole genre. William Fuller Pocock's *Architectural Designs for Rustic Cottages, Picturesque Dwellings, Villas &c* (1807) contains plans for a whole range of estate buildings, from a three-room labourer's cottage consisting of living-kitchen, wash-house and single bedroom, through more spacious accommodation for bailiffs, woodsmen, huntsmen and stewards, to full-size mansions 'in the antient English style'. In his introduction Pocock distinguishes between the 'habitations of the Labourer' and the '*Cabâne Ornée*, or ornamented Cottage'. A landlord building the former will serve the cause of humanity (and, by providing a small garden for them to work, distract his tenants from 'spending their time and money in scenes of intemperance, whereby their habits of industry are relaxed, and their morals corrupted'). He will also delight the eye:

> *When the mind is filled with beautiful and sublime ideas from the contemplation of an extensive prospect, as the circle of vision gradually contracts, the eye dwells with particular delight on the clay built Cottage covered with thatch; or if embosomed in umbrageous foliage, the roof alone be visible, this with the light and curling smoke will sufficiently enliven the scene . . .*

The ornamented cottage, on the other hand, has to be rather more than just an object of interest in a Morland landscape made real. Though humble in its appearance, it will be a country retreat for a merchant, a shooting box for an aristocrat or the residence of a gentleman of independent fortune in landed property, wishing to farm a part of his own estate. Since such buildings must afford 'the necessary conveniences for persons of refined manners and habits', their design focuses much more clearly on the needs of their occupants rather than on their visual impact in the landscape. There are servants' quarters, conservatories, wine cellars. A verandah shades the owner from the heat of the sun, or provides a useful promenade in wet weather. Trellises support 'the gay luxuriance of the

AN 1807 DESIGN BY ROBERT LUGAR FOR A COTTAGE AND BLACKSMITH'S FORGE.

Passion Flower', and belt-planting of the boundaries gives privacy, while openings in the belt are left to present pleasing or interesting prospects of the surrounding countryside. ('The cottage of a labourer may occupy many situations,' wrote John Wood the younger, 'but that of a gentleman must be secluded.') The owners of one of Pocock's ornamented cottages could retire into a primitive Arcadian idyll, 'unencumbered with the forms of state and troublesome appendages' and surrounded by maids, gardeners, and the latest modern conveniences.

It is hard to tell just how many of these cottages of gentility were ever actually built. None of Malton's executed designs seems to have survived, although in his *British Cottage Architecture* he refers in passing to having built a cottage near London with a rustic porch. Pocock's son, William Willmer Pocock, recorded some thirty-three of his father's works, including *cottages ornées* at Blackheath (for Sir John Eamer, 1811) and at Harting in Sussex. Robert Lugar, whose *Architectural Sketches for Cottages, Rural Dwellings, and Villas* appeared in 1805, executed a number of gentry cottages in the south of England in the 1820s. No doubt a great many *cottages ornées* were built – newspapers of the day are full of advertisements for 'cottages' in the fashionable areas around London. But relatively few have survived. The pleasures of the simple life soon palled, while

WHITE-WASHED, THATCHED COTTAGES AT SELWORTHY IN SOMERSET,

BUILT IN **1828** AND INSPIRED BY JOHN NASH'S WORK AT BLAISE HAMLET.

The furniture and furnishing of cottages have been hitherto neglected in every country where the comfort of the cottager has depended on those above him, and this never can be fully remedied till the inmate of the cottage is sufficiently enlightened to be able to take care of himself. We have shown . . . that all that is essential, in point of the general arrangement of a house, may be obtained in a cottage with mud walls, as well as in a palace built of marble; and we intend now to point out in what manner all that is comfortable, convenient, agreeable and much of even what is elegant, in modern furniture and furnishing, may be formed of the indigenous woods and other common articles of every country, as well as of the most beautiful exotic timbers, and other costly materials obtained from abroad.

GOTHIC-STYLE LOBBY CHAIR

If it should be asked whether we expect that such Designs as those which follow can be executed or procured by the cottagers of this country, we answer that we trust they soon will be. And we believe that the first step towards this desirable end is to teach them what to wish for. As the spread of habits of thinking will go hand in hand with comfortable dwellings, and convenient, neat, and elegant forms of furniture. An approximation to equalisation in knowledge will lead to an approximation in every thing else; for knowledge is power, and the first use which every man makes of it is, to endeavour to better his own condition. Our grand object, therefore, in this as in every other department of our work,

DRESSER IN THE GOTHIC STYLE

is to cooperate with the causes at present in operation for bettering the condition, and elevating the character, of the great mass of society in all countries.

Though most of the Designs submitted are of a superior description to what are common in cottages, they are not on that account more expensive than various cumbrous articles of furniture now possessed or desired by every cottager in tolerable circumstances. The difference will be found to consist chiefly in the kind of labour employed in making them, and in the style of design which they exhibit. To speak in familiar language, we have given more work for the joiner than for the carpenter; and our Designs pretend to nothing more than what could be invented by any joiner who could read and draw, and derive ideas from books . . .

Chairs may be classed as suitable for the lobby, kitchen, parlour, and bedroom . . . A lobby chair of wood in the Grecian style may be made of deal, with the exception of the legs, which, being turned, should be of

LONGCASE CLOCK

beech or some fine-grained wood suitable for that operation. This chair may be painted of the colour of the wall against which it is to stand. A lobby chair in the Gothic style may be made entirely of deal, or of any other common wood, and painted and grained in imitation of oak. A Windsor chair is one of the best kitchen chairs in general use in the midland counties of England. The seat is of elm, somewhat hollowed out; the outer rail of the back is of ash, in one piece, bent to a sort of horseshoe form by being previously heated or steamed; its ends are then inserted

in two holes bored through the seat, and are wedged firmly in from the under side. An additional support is given to the back, by two round rails, which are also made fast in two holes, formed in a projecting part of the seat. These chairs are sometimes painted, but more frequently stained with diluted sulphuric acid and logwood; or by repeatedly washing them over with alum water, which has some tartar in it: they should afterwards be washed over several times with an extract of Brasil wood. The colour given will be sort of red, not unlike that of mahogany; and, by afterwards oiling the chair and rubbing it well, and for a long time with woollen cloths, the veins and shading of the elm will be rendered conspicuous. Quicklime slacked in urine, and laid on the wood while hot, will also stain it of a red colour; and this is said to be the general practice with the Windsor chair manufacturers in the neighbourhood of London . . .

GRECIAN-STYLE LOBBY CHAIR

WINDSOR CHAIR

Dressers are fixtures essential to every kitchen, but more especially to that of the cottager, to whom they serve both as dressers and sideboards. They are generally made of deal by joiners, and seldom painted, it being the pride of good housewives, in most parts of England, to keep the boards of which they are composed as white as snow by frequently scouring them with fine white sand. The dishes, plates, etc., which they contain are also kept perfectly clean and free from dust by being wiped every day, whether used or not. In old farmhouses, the dressers are generally of oak rubbed bright, and the shelves are filled with rows of pewter plates, etc., polished by frequent cleaning till they shine like silver. The dresser may be called the cottager's sideboard, and in the dining rooms of the first noblemen's houses in Britain, the splendid mahogany sideboards, set out with gold and silver plate, differ only in the costliness of the materials employed from the cottage dress-

er: nor do the essentials of human food differ more in the palace and in the cottage than the furniture; for, in Britain and America at least, good meat, good bread, and good potatoes are the main dishes on all tables, and may be obtained by the workman who has good wages and full employment, as well as by the wealthy merchant or hereditary aristocrat . . .

A settle is frequently to be met with in public houses. The back forms an excellent screen or protection from the current of air which is continually passing from the door to the chimney. The drawers below are deep, and will be found very useful for a variety of purposes. On the back there might be a towel roller; or, in a superior kind of cottage, the back of the settle might be ornamented with prints or maps, in the manner of a screen. Placed in the open floor, where it would seldom require to be moved, there might even be book shelves fixed to this back . . .

A sofa is a piece of furniture which affords a great source of comfort to its possessor; and therefore the cottager ought to have one as well as the rich man. Let him strive to obtain it, for no parlour is completely furnished without one; and he will certainly succeed . . . A very cheap and yet tasteful loose sofa cover may be made of glazed self-coloured calico, with a narrow piece of different coloured calico, or shawl bordering, laid on about a couple of inches from the edge . . . In all cases where the covers of sofas are made of a material which admits of a choice of colours, those should be preferred which prevail in the carpet and window curtains of the room; the principal reason in this and all similar cases, being that such a choice indicates unity of design.

SETTLE WITH TWO DRAWERS

FROM *ENCYCLOPAEDIA OF COTTAGE, FARM AND VILLA ARCHITECTURE AND FURNITURE*, BY J. C. LOUDON, 1857.

Victorian earnestness viewed such fripperies with mistrust and a certain contempt.

Greater numbers of self-consciously rustic estate cottages have survived from the late eighteenth and early nineteenth centuries. Especially in the southern counties, one can still see plenty of examples, from the Blaise Hamlet-inspired village of Selworthy in Somerset, where white-washed thatched cottages straggle around a long green, to the five pairs of brick estate cottages by George Dance the younger that line the street at East Stratton in Hampshire. Perhaps such smaller cottages have survived because their owners did not have to live in them, or, more significantly, because they continued to serve not only a visual purpose, but also an ideological one, confirming the 'primitive' nature and therefore the low social status of one's tenants and estate workers.

The extent to which the fashion for rustic cottages affected the life of the cottagers

A LODGE AT FONTHILL IN WILTSHIRE EXEMPLIFIES THE SELF-CONSCIOUSLY RUSTIC.

themselves is hard to gauge. The pensioners at Blaise seem to have taken fairly well to being objects of curiosity, figures in a Picturesque landscape. John Harford's son tells us that his father loved to stroll around the 'sweet little village' he had built, and that 'he met there in every Cottager the beaming expression of gratitude to a kind Benefactor'. But then he would say that, wouldn't he?

In any case, the rustic *cottage ornée* as a suitable retreat for the landed classes was a relatively short-lived phenomenon, an intriguing if bizarre byway rather than a highway in both the history of the English cottage and the history of English architecture as a whole. By the 1820s it had largely been supplanted by Old English vernacular, and its Romantic associations were replaced by a more nationalistic and less primitive vision of the past – Merry England, the age of chivalry and the days of good Queen Bess.

But the vogue for the rustic has a greater significance than its brief popularity might suggest. It represents the first attempt by the property-owning classes to take over the motifs and designs of traditional rural worker-housing. After the workmanlike and down-to-earth designs for labourers' cottages that John Wood published in the 1780s, the plethora of rustic cottages that followed seem like either charming fantasies or absurd extravagances, depending on one's point of view. Nevertheless, the work of Nash, Pocock, Malton and their contemporaries had created among the educated upper and middle classes an interest in the cottage as a building type.

That interest was taken up and amplified by perhaps the most influential figure in the history of the early-nineteenth-century cottage – the farmer, landscape designer and writer on agricultural improvement John Claudius Loudon. Loudon was born in Lanarkshire in 1783. After training as a landscape gardener he set up practice in London in 1803, and the following year published *Observations on the Formation and Management of Useful and Ornamental Plantations*, the first in a string of books and tracts on agriculture, horticulture and landscape design, intended to capitalize on the passion of early-nineteenth-century landowners for improving their estates. His pamphlet describing *An Immediate and Effectual Mode of Raising the Rental of the Landed Property of England* (1808) aroused a great deal of interest among landowners eager to increase their income. As a result of that work, Loudon was invited by General Stratton to manage his 1,500-acre estate at Tew Park in Oxfordshire, where Loudon set up one of the first agricultural colleges in the country. The college was closed in 1811, and Loudon then travelled abroad in eastern Europe before branching out as an editor and writer. The

publication of his *Encyclopaedia of Gardening* in 1822 established his reputation as one of the leading British writers on horticulture.

Loudon suffered a number of setbacks in his life, any one of which might have brought a lesser man's career to a halt. He lost all his money through rash speculation. He was severely disabled by rheumatoid arthritis in his left knee. He suffered a bout of laudanum addiction, and in 1825 his right arm, which had been weakened by the same rheumatic fever that had crippled his leg, had to be amputated. (There is an apocryphal story that before he lost his arm, Loudon's handwriting was so much affected by the fever that when he wrote to the Duke of Wellington asking to be allowed to see the famous Waterloo beeches at Stratfield Saye, the Duke read the signature on the letter as 'London', and fired off a gruff note to the Bishop of London telling him he had no idea why the Bishop should want to see the breeches he wore at Waterloo.) Yet these disasters did little to check Loudon's career. By the time of his death in 1843 he had published more than thirty works, ranging from three further encyclopedias – on plants, trees and shrubs and agriculture – to plans for a national educational establishment, and notes on 'the different modes of cultivating the pineapple'.

The trend towards more profitable farming methods went hand in hand with a more active and responsible interest in the living conditions of the rural labourer, just as, following Price, Knight, Nash and Malton, the pursuit of the Picturesque encompassed buildings as well as landscape. As a product of and propagandist for both agricultural improvement and the landscape movement, Loudon's interests inevitably widened during

ESTATE COTTAGES AT CONOCK MANOR IN WILTSHIRE, BUILT *C.* 1820 AT THE HEIGHT OF THE CRAZE FOR *COTTAGES ORNÉES.*

the 1820s to include architecture as well as farming and botany. 'Though we are not a practising architect,' he wrote in 1831, 'yet we pretend to as thorough a knowledge of the principles of architecture, as of those of land-scape-gardening.' The previous year he had brought his horticultural, agricultural and architectural interests together in a short tract entitled *A Manual of Cottage Husbandry, Gardening and Architecture*. In 1833 this essay was incorporated in one of his most influential architectural works – the *Encyclopaedia of Cottage, Farm and Villa Architecture and Furniture*.

The first 350 pages of Loudon's compendious encyclopedia consist of designs 'for labourers' and mechanics' cottages, and for dwellings of gardeners and bailiffs, and other upper servants, and for small farmers and cultivators of their own land'. At the bottom end of the range is 'A Dwelling for a Man and his Wife, without Children' – a single-storey cottage consisting of a combined parlour, dining room and bedroom measuring twelve by twelve feet. Set back to either side of this block are two projecting 'wings'. One contains a wash-house, 'which must also serve as a store-room, pantry, and for various other purposes; the other forms the porch, where fuel and 'tools of husbandry' are stored, with access from the back to a privy. For the more ambitious landlord or speculative builder, there are plans for 'A Dwelling of Two Stories, for a Man and his Wife, with a Servant and Two or Three Children, with a Cow-house and Pigsty', 'A Cottage Dwelling with Two Sitting-Rooms, in the Old English Manner' and 'A Cottage Dwelling in the German Swiss Style, for a Man and his Family, with Accommodation for two Horses and a Cow'. All in all there are eighty-one sets of plans and elevations, each one meticulously described and priced. The single-storey cottage for the childless couple is estimated at between £50 and £100, depending on the price per foot of walling.

Such a detailed collection of cottage plans offers an insight into the ideal that landowners and builders were being exhorted to aim for in the early nineteenth century. Loudon's aim in bringing these designs together was to provide ideas for the housing of

A MULTIPLICITY OF MOTIFS

AND DESIGNS FROM J. C.

LOUDON'S *COTTAGE, FARM AND*

VILLAGE ARCHITECTURE, 1857.

what he describes as 'the lower and middling classes of society'. (Although some were his own, many were the work of outside contributors, and the *Encyclopaedia*'s editor was quick to suggest improvements to the originals – a parapet here, a taller chimney stack there.) They are, he says, 'the beau ideal of what we think every married couple, having children of both sexes, and living in the country, should possess . . . In such dwellings every labourer ought to live, and ' – stretching a point, this – 'any nobleman might live'.

In spite of a somewhat eclectic approach to style – the castellated lodges, the Old English and 'German Swiss' – many of the cottage designs have elements in common. Combining functional convenience with aesthetics, they are almost all raised on an elevated platform, 'with a view of keeping [the living rooms] drier, and consequently, warmer and healthier; as well as to procure greater dignity of effect as an object in the landscape'. They usually place chimneys on the interior rather than exterior walls, to retain the maximum possible heat. And they all contain privies.

One of Loudon's own designs serves as an example for the rest, giving a remarkably detailed picture of his ideal image of rural worker-housing. His optimistically titled 'Cottage of One Story, combining all the Accommodation and Conveniencies of which human Dwellings of that description are susceptible', is raised up on a platform walk five feet wide. There is a kitchen-living room (ten feet by thirteen feet, six inches), entered via a covered porch, a connecting parlour (ten by eleven feet) equipped with a fireplace standing back-to-back with that in the living-kitchen and three bedrooms. (Loudon notes that the parlour will rarely need a fire lit, since 'it will receive a good deal of heat from the kitchen fire'.) The largest bedroom (ten feet, six inches by eight feet) is for husband and wife and leads off the living-kitchen. The boys' bedroom is reached through the parlour and that for the girls through their parents' room. None of the bedrooms have fires.

A cellar beneath Loudon's model cottage, reached by steps leading down beside the porch, contains three further rooms. One functions as back-kitchen, wash-house, brewhouse and bake-house, with an oven placed directly under the parlour. A second is a 'store cellar and larder for potatoes, beer, home-made wines, fresh and salt meat, and similar articles of provision'. The third is a combined milk-house and pan-try, the window of which must be of wire or haircloth since both exclude air and heat or cold.

There are two privies. One, access to which is through the girls' bedroom, is 'for the mother, girls, and females'. The basin, says Loudon, 'may be of brown earthenware or of cast iron, so as to cost very little; the door ought to open inwards, and the small window outwards, so that every movement of the door may act as a ventilator'. He also suggests that there may be a wash-handbasin, although it is clear that this is an option rather than an essential requirement. The second privy, the 'man and boy's water-closet', stands in a walled yard behind the cottage. Loudon claims that the provision of two privies, so long as both are water closets as opposed to earth closets, is justified not only on the grounds of cleanliness and decency, but also because the liquid manure thus gained will be useful in the garden. It collects in one of two enclosed cesspools in the yard – two, because the manure should be fermented before use, so it becomes necessary to be able to switch sewage to one pit when the other is full.

Besides the privy and the cesspools, the yard is also surrounded by accommodation for an assortment of livestock. There is a cow-house, a pigsty and a place for ducks or geese 'with a small poultry-stair or ladder to hen-loft above it'. A projecting alcove at the side of the cottage contains shelves for beehives, with a dovecote above and a kennel for the family's dog beneath. Loudon even specifies a large cornice to the chimney, 'for the purpose of encouraging swallows to build their nests there; these birds being of great importance to cultivators and possessors of gardens, as destroyers of winged insects, on which they live entirely'.

The *Encyclopaedia* goes into great detail about the need for every cottage to have an independent water supply and advocates the collection of rainwater as a primary source. Loudon's model cottage contains one tank for cooking purposes, with water filtered through a bed of either sand and charcoal or coarse burnt clay, and a larger tank for the water-closets, the animals, and for washing and cleaning. A rotary pump draws water from this main tank, while a cast-iron box with a lid is set into the kitchen floor above the oven in the cellar, so that the cottagers can keep a permanent supply of domestic hot water on hand. The flue from this oven snakes across below the floor of the cottage, providing a simple form of underfloor heating. Loudon argues the 'immense superiority' of this mode of heating, on the grounds that with more conventional fires and hot-water pipes, the coldest layer of air is always to be found at floor level, whereas with his system, 'the lowest stratum is necessarily the hottest, which must be preferable for the feet and legs of grown persons, and for the whole bodies of little children'.

In elevation, the model cottage is plain enough – no undulating roofline or quaint brick-filled timber-framing. (Variations on the basic design, however, did include steeply overhanging thatch supported by rustic poles.) The apparently workmanlike functionalism of Loudon's scheme is unbroken by any planting – he allows that fruit trees, vines, roses and honeysuckle might be trained up the side walls, but 'there is a danger of indulging in these to such an extent as to keep the walls damp, and to encourage flies and other insects'. The austere outline is relieved only by the low platform on which the cottage perches, giving it a certain dignity, and by what seems at first sight to be a rather formal pedimented porch. Even this detail has a clear function: Loudon has recommended the space above the beehives on the side wall be kept for doves, but in this instance he suggests the dovecote is placed in the pediment.

The materials used for the cottage are left to the builder's discretion. The walls may be of stone, brick or earth, although Loudon suggests that earth, less durable and less strong than the other two, is only employed as a last resort if stone and brick are considered too expensive. The roof can be tiled, thatched or slated, and the bill for the construction work will come to a grand total of between £210 and £420, depending on the choice of materials. These are daunting figures considering that the agricultural labourer's average weekly earnings in the mid-nineteenth century were somewhere around ten or eleven shillings, with perhaps another four shillings brought in by his wife and children.

Of course Loudon's designs were not aimed at the agricultural labourer himself. They were meant for the speculative builder and, more importantly, the landowner, who was under increasing pressure from moral and sanitary reformers to provide decent housing for his tenants and estate workers. Even so, Loudon's model cottage would be a bad investment. It was generally held at the time that gross rent needed to be about ten per cent of capital costs in order to cover repairs and rates and to yield a small profit, so Loudon's figures would imply an annual rent of between £21 and £42. Yet average rentals were only about £4 per annum, giving a return of around 0.95% or 1.9%, depending on materials used. Even his cheapest single-room cottage, built at a cost of £50-£100, would only yield between four and eight per cent.

The sense of unease at the practicality of a labourer actually living in one of Loudon's cottages, a feeling that the author is out of touch with the realities of rural life, begins to grow when one turns to the section of the *Encyclopaedia* that deals with 'Designs and Directions for Exterior and Interior Finishing, as connected with Furnishing, and for the Fittings-up, Fixtures, and Furniture of Cottage Dwellings'.

A composition for exterior colouring. Take 26 pounds of quicklime, slacked to a powder, and well sifted, and 28 pounds of tarras, sifted well. Mix these with a small quantity of water as quickly as possible. Beat them together with a wooden beater, upon a banker (a stone or wooden bench). Continue to beat them three or four times a day, for four days; and, at the end of that period, take three gallons of bullock's blood (which should be well stirred in the catching, to prevent it clotting), and add to it, when cold, three gallons of water. Put the lime and tarras into a tub, together with the blood and water, stirring them well to make the wash thin; when it will be fit for use. Keep stirring while using it, to prevent the tarras from settling at the bottom. Let the wall be first cleaned from moss and dirt, washing it twice with a watering-pot; and, before it is dry, begin to lay on the composition, observing not to work it too thick. In the second washing, add two quarts more blood, properly stirred while cooling, as before, to make the wash more sizy and glutinous. If a yellow tinge be desired, put in a pound or more of stone or Roman ochre. Stale milk may be substituted for blood, though it is said by some not to make the wash resist the weather equally well.

The doors of cottages may be ornamented by adding strips of deal, in the form of muntins, styles, rails, beads, etc., by ornamental hinges and latches; or by studding them over with imitation door nails. The plain door may be rendered architectural in the Gothic style at a very trifling expense by fillets nailed on so as to produce the

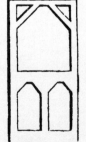

effect, or by nails. The woodwork should be painted in imitation of oak, and the heads of the nails should be black. These nails are to be procured complete, of different shapes, in cast iron; but they are equally fit for producing effect when the heads are made of wood, and fastened on by a brad. The heads of these nails may be round, square, triangular, or polygonal; and with either flat or raised surfaces. Ornamental hinges, or plates of iron into which ornamental nails are driven, may also be imitated in wood, and completely disguised by paint; as may be certain parts of common latches, the es-cutcheons of key-holes, etc. All knobs to cottage doors should be of real oak, laburnum (false ebony, as it is called by the French, from its hardness and blackness), yew, box, or other hard and tough wood, or of iron blackened or bronzed, but never of brass, which is too fine, and is besides liable to tarnish.

In the choice of patterns for stenciling, not only the architectural style of the cottage, but its situation, whether in a town, the country or in a village; and the occupation, native country, and taste or wishes, of the occupant, will naturally influence the artist. As contrast is one great source of beauty, . . . so figures of flowers and plants in gay colours are more suitable for the town than the country, and figures of human beings, buldings, and streets, are more suitable for the country than for the town . . .

The colouring of the walls of rooms with water colours, or in what is called distemper . . . All the different colours are used for the walls of rooms; but the most common, after white, are some shades of yellow, red, green, or grey. As a general rule, the ceiling should be of a lighter colour than the walls; because it is found that, when it is darker, it is apparently brought nearer to the eye, and has con-

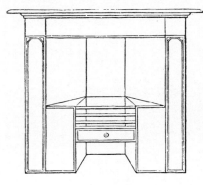

sequently the effect of making the room appear low. Rooms which are too low may on the same principle be made to appear somewhat higher than they are, by having the walls a shade darker than is usual, and the ceilings a shade lighter, and this effect may be heightened by a slight gradation in the shade of the wall from the base to the cornice.

Painting the internal woodwork of cottages ought never to be neglected, both on account of its preservative quality and its ornamental effect. All woodwork, avowed as such, should, if possible, be grained in imitation of some natural wood; not with a view of having the imitation mistaken for the original, but rather to create allusion to it, and, by a diversity of lines and shades, to produce a kind of variety and intricacy, which affords more pleasure to the eye than a flat shade of colour. The most suitable colour for the woodwork of cottages is undoubtedly that of the prevailing timber of the district or country in which the cottage is built; at the same time, where this timber is but slightly veined or marked, it is allowable and advisable to imitate a better description of wood. Thus, in England, the prevailing timber in several districts is fir and poplar; but, as the wood of these trees is much inferior in beauty to that of the oak, the elm, or the chestnut, which respectively prevail in different parts of Britain, it would be allowable, and what would be considered in good taste, for the painter to imitate them.

Curtains for the humblest description of Cottages. Where an apparatus of lines and pulleys would be too expensive, a simple curtain, opening in the centre, may be formed by nailing two pieces of dimity, coloured calico, or printed cotton, to a square cornice, either painted, or covered with a piece of paper bordering; these curtains may be looped back by a piece of sash line, or coloured cord, twisted round hooks fixed to the architrave, and will thus form a kind of Gothic drapery across the window.

Chimney-pieces for the kitchens of cottages should generally be finished with stone facings and stone shelves; but, where the stone is sandy and brittle, it is much better to substitute stout shelves of deal or oak. The cottage parlour should, if possible, have a marble chimney-piece; and those of the bedrooms may be of stone or composition.

Paper Carpets are formed by cutting out and sewing together pieces of linen, cotton, Scotch gauze, canvas, or any similar material, etc., to the size and form required; then stretching the prepared cloth on the floor of a large room, and carefully pasting it round the margins so as to keep it strained tight. When the cloth thus fixed is dry, lay on it two or more coats of strong paper, and finish with coloured or hanging paper, according to fancy. Centre or corner pieces, cut out of remnants of papers, which may be bought for a mere trifle, may be laid on a self-coloured ground, and the whole surrounded by a border, or any other method adopted which may suit the taste or circumstances of the occupier. When the carpet is thus prepared, and quite dry, it should receive two coats of glue, or size made from the shreds of skins, such as is used by carvers and gilders. When the size is perfectly dry, the carpet should have one or more coats of boiled oil; and when that is dry, a coat of copal or any other varnish. These carpets are portable and will roll up with about the same ease as oil-cloth. They are very durable, are easily cleaned; and, if made of well-chosen patterns, have a very handsome appearance.

FROM *ENCYCLOPAEDIA OF COTTAGE, FARM AND VILLA ARCHITECTURE AND FURNITURE*, BY J. C. LOUDON, 1857.

His advice on exterior finishes is straightforward enough, with suggestions for stucco, roughcast, lime and hair plaster and whitewash, although his concern that 'the parts and finishing of the exterior . . . ought to convey to us some ideas of the taste of the occupant' might seem a rather ambitious view of rural vernacular housing. But this taste veers more and more towards the ornamental as the chapter wears on. Plain doors can be 'rendered architectural, in the Gothic style' by nailing on fillets; lattice windows can be disguised with Gothic framework; iron door furniture should be blackened by heating it until it is nearly red hot, plunging it in oil, and then polishing with coarse woollen cloth.

Once we arrive inside Loudon's cottages, their essentially bourgeois nature is immediately apparent. The internal walls of a cottage 'of the humblest class' may need no other finishing than rubbing down and dressing with a single coat of plaster. Nevertheless 'without a cornice no room can have a finished appearance, therefore we recommend cornices to be introduced into the living-rooms and principal bed-rooms of even the humblest cottages.' From the necessary introduction of a cornice, it is a short step to plaster ornaments on ceilings – 'a rose or other flower, in plaster or composition, might often be introduced, at very little expense, in the centre of the ceiling of a cottage parlour'.

On to the fixtures and furniture. There are Gothic fireplaces, Grecian dressers and cast-iron Etruscan lobby chairs. There are bookcases, escritoires and bureaux, all 'extremely useful for holding books, keeping papers, or writing on; therefore no cottage

A COTTAGE OF CONTENTMENT?

ALMSHOUSE AT AYNHO IN NORTHHAMPTONSHIRE, 1846.

parlour ought to be without one'. There are sofas on castors, half-tester beds and elaborately draped 'French' beds, 'generally formed like couch beds, especially those in use by French cottagers', Loudon says rather desperately'. He even gives designs for two clock cases – one Grecian, one Gothic – suggesting that clock cases for cottages may be harmonized both with the style of the building and that of the other furniture, 'by the lines of their mouldings and the forms of their panels'.

Loudon's *Encyclopaedia* found its way onto the shelves of most mid-nineteenth-century architects' and builders' offices, helping to set the tone for smaller-scale building and interior decoration in England for much of the early Victorian period. In fact, looking back at the 1830s and 1840s it is tempting to blame Loudon for all that is tasteless, imitative and stylistically naive in early Victorian design, all the mass-produced, badly designed artefacts that crowded the Great Exhibition of 1851. 'We have parish paupers smoking their pipes and drinking their beer under Gothic arches and sculptured niches,' wrote a contributor to *The Architectural Magazine* in 1837, 'and quiet old English gentlemen . . . peeping out of Swiss chalets.' That contributor was the young John Ruskin.

But was Loudon seeking to give the cottage over to the burgeoning middle classes, who lapped up his ideas for Gothic hat stands, umbrella stands and washstands? Or was he simply trying to raise the standard of worker-housing? He clearly thought that he was doing the latter:

> *If it should be asked, whether we expect that such Designs as those which follow can be executed or procured by the cottagers of this country, we answer that we trust they soon will be; and we believe that the first step towards this desirable end is, to teach them what to wish for. As the spread of knowledge becomes general, it will be accompanied by the spread of taste; and correct habits of thinking will go hand in hand with comfortable dwellings, and convenient, neat, and elegant forms of furniture.*

But if Loudon's motives were laudable, his real failure lay in not appreciating the true state of the English cottage in the middle years of the century. He thought, as so many of his contemporaries did, that improving the lot of the labouring classes meant no more than telling them what to do, imposing essentially middle-class values and behaviour patterns. To him it was all a matter of instilling the correct taste.

In 1849, six years after Loudon's death, Alexander Mackay described his experience of a typical Buckinghamshire two-room cottage in an article in the *Morning Chronicle*:

> *On leaving the bright light without, the room which you enter is so dark that for a time you can with difficulty discern the objects which it contains . . . At one corner stands a small ricketty table, whilst scattered about are three old chairs – one without a back – and a stool or two, which, with a very limited and imperfect washing apparatus, and a shelf or two for plates, tea-cups, &c,*

constitute the whole furniture of the apartment . . .

[The bedroom is] gained by means of a few greasy and ricketty steps, which lead through a species of hatchway in the ceiling. Yes, there is but one room, and yet we counted nine in the family! And such a room! The small window in the roof admits just light enough to discern its character and dimensions. The rafters, which are all exposed, spring from the very floor, so that it is only in the very centre of the apartment that you have any chance of standing erect. The thatch oozes through the woodwork which supports it, the whole being begrimed with smoke and dust, and replete with vermin . . . You look in vain for a bedstead; there is none in the room. But there are their beds, lying side by side on the floor almost in contact with each other, and occupying nearly the whole length of the apartment. The beds are large sacks filled with the chaff of oats.

Try telling that unnamed family to develop their taste, that their lives would be improved immeasurably if they owned a Gothic umbrella stand or a cast-iron Etruscan lobby chair. Theirs was the real cottage England. And it was their plight – and their cottages – that were to exercise the minds of reformers and social commentators for the remainder of the nineteenth century.

IMPROVISING: THE WOMAN MAKING OATCAKES IN THIS YORKSHIRE COTTAGE HAS MADE A DRYING RACK FROM AN OVERTURNED CHAIR AND A PIECE OF CLOTH.

CHAPTER V

The
Deserving Poor
1840-1900

The cottage-homes of England! Yes, I know
How picturesque their moss and weather-stain,
Their golden thatch, whose squared eaves shadows throw
On white-washed wall and deep-sunk lattice pane . . .
All these I know – know, too, the plagues that prey
On those who dwell in these bepainted bowers:
The foul miasma of their crowded rooms,
Unaired, unlit, with green damps moulded o'er,
The fever that each autumn deals its dooms
From the rank ditch that stagnates by the door;
And then I wish the picturesqueness less,
And welcome the utilitarian hand
That from such foulness plucks its masquing dress,
And bids the well-aired, well-drained cottage stand,
All bare of weather-stain, right-angled true,
By sketches shunned, but shunned by fevers too.

TOM TAYLOR, 'OLD COTTAGES', 1863

Picture the scene. An overgrown country lane, and behind a flower-filled hedge an ancient, stone-built cottage, its brick chimneys rising high above the deep-set windows that poke through the quaint, uneven thatch. A fresh-faced young girl dressed in bonnet and pinafore leans against an open gate, cradling a kitten in her arms and gazing demurely out, while the kitten's mother waits alert at her feet. Cottage and foliage surround the child, keeping her as safe in their arms as the kitten is in hers.

Helen Allingham's 1898 painting *A Dorsetshire Cottage* is emblematic of the Victorians' love affair with the cottage. She began her career as a magazine illustrator, working on *The Graphic* and *The Cornhill*. In 1874 she married the Irish nature-poet William Allingham, and seven years later the couple moved to Witley in Surrey, where Helen began to specialize in the pictures of cottages for which she is best remembered today. In painting after painting, clean, fresh-faced little girls in pinafores and bonnets stand at the gates of their cottages, clutching kittens or wicker baskets. Mothers with babes in arms keep a careful eye on their offspring from the doorway, geese and ducks troop down the lane before them, while doves nestle in the thatch and hens peck in the dirt. In the words of her admirer Stuart Dick, whose *Cottage Homes of England* Allingham illustrated:

Her England is a sunny England, her cottages are happy homes . . . The gar-
den is full of flowers, the sun shines with a cool and tempered light, and the
whole scene breathes of peacefulness. There is no jarring note. Where the mod-
ern occupier has erected an ugly iron railing, or cut through the beams of the
framework in enlarging a window, or added a corrugated iron roof to a lean-
to, a judicious restoration has taken place, and we see the cottage not as it
unfortunately now is, but as it used to be.

HELEN ALLINGHAM'S *A DORSETSHIRE COTTAGE*, THE EPITOME OF THE
VICTORIAN LOVE AFFAIR WITH IDYLLIC COUNTRY LIFE.

THE LESS ROMANTIC REALITY BEHIND ALLINGHAM'S VISION

These 'judiciously' restored cottages, drawn mainly in the countryside of Surrey and Kent, form part of a genre that reached its peak at the end of the nineteenth century. Helen Allingham and her neighbour and contemporary Myles Birket Foster are perhaps its two most famous exponents. There are plenty of other painters of the genre, however: Charles Low and Charles Edward Wilson, Samuel Towers, who made a speciality of painting Cotswold scenes, and Helen Allingham's sister, Caroline Sharpe, whose works were described as 'delights to the eye and lasting memorials of the fast-vanishing beauty of our countryside . . . no false mirages but beautiful truth'.

The idea that the England depicted by the cottage painters of the Witley School and their contemporaries was fast disappearing is key to an understanding of Victorian idealizations of the cottage. The early-nineteenth-century Romantic notion of the countryside had been given new impetus by industrialization. Families had flocked towards work in the cities in their hundreds of thousands. By the time of the 1851 census the balance between urban and rural populations, which had always favoured the countryside, had finally shifted towards the town, and over the next decades that shift continued so that by 1881 the urban figures were double those of the rural.

But the growth of the cities brought with it poverty and squalor, and helped to create a population that felt alienated, cut off from its roots in the country, cast out of Eden. Thomas Carlyle fulminated that 'men are grown mechanical in head and in heart, as well as in hand'. John Ruskin spoke out against the social effects of the Industrial Revolution, saying that 'there might be more freedom in England, though her feudal lords' lightest words were worth men's lives, and though the blood of the vexed husbandman dropped in the furrows of her fields, than there is while the animation of her multitudes is sent like fuel to feed the factory smoke'. And William Morris dreamt of a utopian future in which towns were swept away and England was become 'a garden . . . with all the necessary

THE RURAL ENGLISH VILLAGE PROMPTED IDYLLIC VISIONS FROM 19TH-

CENTURY ARTISTS SUCH AS MYLES BIRKET FOSTER.

Cottage life as depicted by Myles Birket Foster: continuity, calm and closeness to Nature, the antithesis to life in the city.

dwellings, sheds, and workshops scattered up and down the country, all trim and neat and pretty'.

One obvious consequence of the Victorian rejection of the industrial landscape and its values was a growing feeling that the countryside was indeed a paradise, everything that the ugly, overcrowded city was not. 'Those who dwell amidst the vulgar and impossible artistry of modern villadom,' wrote the architect Baillie Scott, 'may visit now and then some ancient village, and in the cottages and farmhouses there be conscious of a beauty which makes their own homes appear a trivial and frivolous affair.' The old country cottages with their happy, contented occupants that were so lovingly depicted – or rather, invented, by Allingham, Birket Foster and their circle – represented for the Victorians certain values that had been lost to progress: stability, tradition, continuity, calm and a closeness to Nature that was the antithesis of life in the big industrial conurbation, with its teeming tenements and grinding poverty. As new railways snaked through previously unspoiled valleys and dales, as the ever-expanding towns reached out to cover the open fields with factories and rows of modern housing, there was a sense that this older, better, more innocent England was disappearing. And that made people value it all the more.

Potent though they are as images of Victorian rural life, the dream cottages depicted in the art of the later nineteenth century represent only one end of the wide spectrum of attitudes towards rural worker-housing. We can glimpse the other end by picturing a cottage drawn from an 1893 report on housing in Essex made by Dr John Thresh, an assistant agricultural commissioner. Thresh shows us another thatched and timber-framed cottage, but unlike Allingham, who concentrates unwaveringly on exterior, he takes us behind the front door. The walls, of lath and plaster or a mixture of clay and chopped straw, are unlined on the inside and less than one inch thick. The downstairs floors are of brick laid directly onto bare earth, and bits of board and layers of sacking cover the areas where the brick has broken and cracked, in an unsuccessful attempt to keep out the damp. Like our first cottage, this too has leaded windows. They do not open, but this scarcely matters, since the frames are so loose that plenty of air comes in around the sides. The window at the back of the house has fallen out, and a piece of matting hangs over the opening. The doors, made of simple

planking, do not fit either, and strips of wood have been nailed along the edges of the doorways and over cracks in the doors themselves to keep out the draughts. The single downstairs room has a fireplace, the only one in the cottage, consisting of a few iron bars set into brickwork. The bricks at the back of the fireplace have cracked and crumbled, and the wide chimney allows more air in from outside than smoke going out.

The ceiling is low – between six and six and a half feet – and unfinished, so that there are gaps showing where the floorboards of the bedroom floor above have broken. These holes have been covered with pieces of wood and old iron, to prevent the bed from falling through. There is no oven, no copper, no sink, no water supply except for polluted ponds and ditches nearby. A communal bakehouse with a brick oven has been built to serve a number of cottages, but this has fallen into disrepair, and is now put to use as a storeroom for wood.

Thresh's cottage is the depressing counterpart to Helen Allingham's idyllic pictures, the Magdalen to her Madonna. Thresh and men like him, social reformers and philanthropists, went beneath the surface of rural life and determined to change what they saw there – poverty every bit as stark and dreadful as that in the slums of Manchester and London. From them we get a more vivid if far less congenial picture of life in the Victorian cottage.

A concern for the problems of the rural poor, and for their housing needs in particular, had been growing steadily throughout the later eighteenth and early nineteenth centuries. In 1781 John Wood was appalled at 'the miserable condition of the poor cottager'. Fifty years later William Cobbett noted with approbation the labourers' dwelling he saw in the Vale of Gloucester, which 'looked good, and the labourers themselves pretty well as to dress and healthiness'. The cottages of Sussex were also 'good and warm; and the gardens some of the best I have seen in England'. But Cobbett, like Wood, was more often moved to rage, exclaiming, 'Look at these hovels, made of mud and straw, bits of glass or of old cast-off windows, without frames or hinges frequently. Enter them and look at the bits of chairs and stools, the wretched boards tacked together to form a table.' Farmworkers lived worse than animals: 'Dogs and hogs and horses are treated with more civility, and as to food and lodging, how gladly would the labourers change for them!' The

A COTTAGE ON THE FELBRIGG ESTATE IN NORFOLK, 1860.

THE REAL VICTORIAN COUNTRY COTTAGE CONTAINED POVERTY EVERY BIT

AS DISTURBING AS THE SLUMS OF MANCHESTER OR LONDON.

same point was made in 1842 by a Berwickshire surveyor, James Cunningham, who found 'the barns and stables, for instance, are always finished more carefully; in these the walls are plastered, the roof and wood-work close and complete, and the floors either boarded or carefully paved.'

One reason for the poor state of cottages was that there simply weren't enough of them. A growing tendency for farmers to follow the manners of the gentry made them reluctant to continue the traditional practice of having their farmworkers living in with them. It was thought better to provide them with separate houses, often no more than hovels, or to pay slightly higher wages and leave the labourer to find his own accommodation. This led to more pressure on the rural housing stock, a pressure that was accentuated by falling mortality rates in the countryside. At the same time, farmers had little incentive to repair or rebuild cottages, especially when the land they occupied could be put to more profitable uses. In 1880 F. G. Heath described an encounter with John, a Somerset farmworker who had lived in a rented single-storey, two-room cottage of mud and thatch for a quarter of a century. Out of his wages of five shillings a week, John paid fifty shillings annual rent for his home, fifteen shillings more for one-eighth of an acre of potato ground, and a further ten shillings for the privilege of grazing his pig on his master's land. 'John said that when his cottage became no longer fit – according to his idea of fitness – for a "residence", the "master" intended to pull down the mud walls and plough up the site.'

When William Cobbett was taking his 'rural rides' in the 1820s, the official response to the relief of the rural poor was in a confused state, varying wildly from one part of the country to another, and even from one parish to another. The 1662 Act of Settlement had enabled parish officers to forcibly return paupers to the parish where they were last legally settled. This law had been supplemented by a further Act in 1722 that sought to set aside outdoor relief – the principle that paupers should be given assistance by the parish in their own homes – in favour of the workhouse system. But this Act, never enforced particularly effectively in rural areas, was itself replaced in 1795 by another which restored outdoor relief.

The 'relief' took various forms. There was 'parish employment', whereby the able-bodied were employed on communal work projects such as road repairs. This was little used since, as one Victorian source put it, 'the method afforded no direct profit to any individual, the labourers could not be properly looked after, and they were invariably lazy and unwilling to do more than they were obliged'. In the 'labour rate' system farmers agreed to take on extra workers in return for having their parish rates reduced. Then there was the 'roundsman' system, an example of which is given in the 1797 edition of Sir Frederick Eden's *The State of the Poor*:

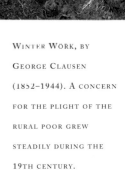

> *[At Winslow in Berkshire] there seems to be a great want of employment: most of the labourers are (as it is termed), on the Rounds; that is, they go to work from one house to another round the parish. In winter sometimes 40 persons are on the rounds. They are wholly paid by the parish, unless the householders choose to employ them; and from these circumstances, labourers often become very lazy, and imperious. Children, above ten years old, are put on the rounds, and receive from the parish from 1s.6d to 3s. a week.*

WINTER WORK, BY GEORGE CLAUSEN (1852–1944). A CONCERN FOR THE PLIGHT OF THE RURAL POOR GREW STEADILY DURING THE 19TH CENTURY.

But by far the most famous device for poor relief (or, to Georgian social commentators, the most notorious) was the Speenhamland system, named after a group of local Justices and landowners who met, to 'limit, direct, and appoint the wages of day labourers', at the Pelican Inn at Speenhamland in Berkshire in May 1795. Speenhamland parishes fixed what a labourer's wages should be, often according to the size of his family and a rough cost of living scale, and he could count on those wages whatever happened. If he was out of work, he could claim the whole amount, and if his pay fell below the threshold, it was supplemented.

TWO DORSET COTTAGERS, FROM THOMAS HARDY'S COLLECTION. 'INTO
THESE WRETCHED HABITATIONS CROWD THE AGRICULTURAL LABOURERS OF
ENGLAND.' – SIR JOHN SIMON

Although the Speenhamland system was nowhere near as widespread as contemporaries believed, especially after high prices during the Napoleonic Wars had begun to fall, it contributed to a growing dissatisfaction among taxpayers with the state of poor relief. Farmers, it was said, were able to offer lower pay, secure in the knowledge that other ratepayers would be forced to contribute to making up the difference. Able-bodied labourers, on the other hand, were being given money for doing nothing. There was little incentive for them to work hard and improve themselves, and they were being encouraged to take pauper wives and have huge families as a way of increasing their allowances. Both the arguments and the low opinion of the poor are depressingly familiar. Poverty was a symptom of individual moral failure rather than social and economic circumstances, a point tellingly made by the title of one Victorian work on poor relief, *From Pauperism to Manliness*.

The Poor Law Amendment Act of 1834 embodied this view. The Act was passed in the aftermath of a Royal Commission Report on the Poor Laws, itself the result of disquiet among the propertied classes at the amount of money that was being spent on poor relief – around £6.3 million a year in the early 1830s, or about nine shillings for every head of the population in England and Wales. The new Act rejected all forms of outdoor relief for the able-bodied and their families apart from medical relief, relying instead on the workhouse as the primary instrument of support. In the infamous words of the Royal Commission report, care should be taken to ensure that the situation of the individual who entered the workhouse should not be 'really or apparently so eligible as the situation of the independent labourer of the lowest class'.

In fact, this proved impossible. The situation of the independent labourer of the lowest class was often so utterly appalling that even the spartan living conditions of the workhouse, where at least one was given meat twice a week, were an improvement. But the social stigma, the dehumanizing uniforms and cropped hair, the segregation of men and women and the consequent breaking up of families all ensured that given the choice few would swap their cottage, however squalid, for the wards of the local workhouse. A Suffolk countrywoman quoted in the *Morning Chronicle* in 1849 summed up popular revulsion against the system: 'I'd work the flesh off my bones afore I'd be parted and locked up like a felon.'

There is also evidence that in country areas the new Act failed in its intention of

THE EJECTED FAMILY. EVICTION USUALLY MEANT THE WORKHOUSE, AND ALL THE TERRORS THAT IMPLIED.

doing away with outdoor relief, if only on the grounds of cost. The rural boards that were set up to organize the new system quickly realized that it might cost twice as much to keep a family in the workhouse as it did to support them in their own homes. Consequently, the letter of the law was often disregarded, with boards doctoring their returns by disguising income support for the low paid as short-term medical relief.

During the Victorian period the schemes like the Poor Law Amendment Act, which set up a Royal Commission to enquire into a problem, became the established means of investigating social ills, and it is from such reports that much of our less anecdotal information about life in the poorer cottages comes. A Poor Law Commissioners' Report of 1843, for example, painted a vivid picture of the state of agricultural labourers' cottages at the bottom end of the scale. At Stourpaine in Dorset a commissioner found a cottage occupied by eleven people. All slept in a single bedchamber in the roof space, ten feet square, with a single window about fifteen inches square. The father and mother slept in one bed, with Jeremiah, an eighteen-month-old toddler, and a baby of four months. A second bed was occupied by two twenty-year-old twins, Sarah and Elizabeth, and their four-year-old sister, Mary. The third bed accommodated the four sons – Silas, aged seventeen, John fifteen, James fourteen and Elias ten. This overcrowding was not unusual for Dorset, says the commissioner: he came across one cottage near Blandford which housed twenty-nine people, and plenty of cases where whole families occupied a single room. The 'painful and yet almost inevitable result of such a demoralizing state of things [was] that the number of illegitimate children was very great in the district'. At Stourpaine the cottage described above was one of a row, fronting an open gutter in the street and separated by two or three narrow passages giving access to the ground behind. This ground, which sloped down to the houses,

LAUNDRY DAY, PENZANCE, 1900. INTO THE 20TH CENTURY, COTTAGERS STILL RELIED ON AN OUTSIDE SOURCE FOR WATER.

contained pigstys and 'shallow excavations, the receptacles, apparently, of all the dirt of the families. The matter constantly escaping from the pigstys, etc., is allowed to find its way through the passages between the cottages into the gutter in the street, so that the cottages are nearly surrounded by streams of filth.'

Not surprisingly, given such conditions, disease was rife. Typhus in particular was a major killer. Since it was thought at the time to be caught from exhalations thrown off by the skin of sufferers (hence the most effective measure against it was, according to one late Victorian source, 'an abundant supply of clean, pure air, by which the poison may be oxidized and destroyed, or diluted until it ceases to be operative'), the crowded conditions in which poorer cottage-dwellers lived were seen as a lethal breeding ground. One commissioner describes a three-room cottage in which all ten occupants were suffering from typhus. The daughter-in-law of the family and two of her children had been placed in a thatched outhouse with an earthen floor, with a well and 'a large tub containing pigs' victuals' for company. And 'the following shocking case' was described by the medical officer to the Cerne Poor Law Union in Dorset, James Fox, in 1842:

> *In a family consisting of six persons, two had fever; the mud floor of their cottage was at least one foot below the lane; it consisted of one small room only, in the centre of which stood a foot-ladder reaching to the edge of a platform which extended over nearly one-half of the room, and upon which were placed two beds, with space between them for one person only to stand, whilst the outside of each touched the thatch. The head of one of these beds stood within six inches of the edge of the platform, and in this bed one of my unfortunate patients, a boy about 11 years old, was sleeping with his mother, and in a fit of delirium, jumped over the head of his bed and fell to the ground below, a height of about seven feet. The injury to the head and spine was so serious that he lived a few hours only after the accident. In a cottage fit for the residence of a human being this could not have occurred.*

The image of the rural cottage evoked by such reports is a bleak one. The unremitting catalogues of personal suffering and family tragedy are a world away from the sunny England of Helen Allingham. Many middle-class commentators, motivated by an entirely Victorian brand of moral outrage, were repelled, not by the fact that death, misery and disease were the everyday lot of many of their fellows, but by the lack of decency that life in an overcrowded cottage necessarily involved. A clergyman wrote to the Poor Law Commission in the early 1840s to describe how 'a married woman of thoroughly good character told me a few weeks ago that, on her confinement, so crowded with children is her one room, they are obliged to put her on the floor in the middle of the room that they may pay her the requisite attention'. Even worse, he had recently visited a cottage in which, on three beds in the same room, lay a widow dying of consumption, two unmarried teenaged daughters, and 'a young married couple whom I myself had married two days before'. The vicar leaves us to imagine the rest – death, sex and adolescent girls in the same room.

By the time that the Poor Law Commission investigated rural housing again, in the late 1860s, things were not much better, although the situation varied considerably across the country. In the north wages were higher and jobs in good supply, and the commissioners found that in Durham a farm labourer could earn as much as fifteen shillings a week, with house rent given and an allowance of potatoes, meat and drink during the harvest. In Bedfordshire wages, including a daily beer allowance, might be as high as 13s.6d;

cottage rents ranged from a shilling to 3s.6d. And in Dorset, admittedly a notoriously depressed agricultural area, a labourer might earn only eight shillings a week with a rent-free cottage, or nine shillings without. Rents varied between one and two shillings, and perks might include cider, and perhaps cartage of fuel and a piece of ground to grow potatoes.

At Butcombe in Somerset the Commission described a 'mere lean-to against the wall of another house' in which a man, his wife and their small children lived, with gaps in the open thatch leaving the sky showing through in places. Canon Edward Girdlestone, whose efforts to improve the lot of farm labourers earned him the title of 'The Agricultural Labourers' Friend', reported from Devon, where he was setting up schemes to help workers migrate to the more prosperous milltowns of Lancashire, that 'many so-called cottages are mere ruinous hovels. In visiting the sick I am often obliged to take great care that my legs do not go through the holes in the floor of the sleeping-room to the room below.' The Commissioner in Wiltshire found that the cottage accommodation was deplorable, and pointed to a sort of hierarchy in which estate cottages came out on top, with those built by speculators for rent coming in as bad seconds, and the thatched wattle and cob built by labourers themselves being the worst.

Not surprisingly there was a general drift away from the countryside into the towns, where wages might be twice as high.

VICTORIAN COTTAGERS SUBSISTED ON MEAGRE RATIONS OF POTATOES, VEGETABLES AND BREAD. MEAT, IF THERE WAS ANY, WAS GIVEN TO THE MAN OF THE HOUSE.

Census returns for England and Wales show a figure of 1.27 million employed in agriculture in 1851 declining to less than 650,000 by 1901. But even so, there was an acute shortage of cottages for much of the Victorian period. An 1864 survey showed that over the ten years between 1851 and 1861 there had been an increase of 5.4% in the population of the 821 parishes investigated and a 4.5% decrease in the number of dwellings. The number of occupants per house had risen from 4.4:1 to 4.9:1.

MENDING CLOTHES. TRUE TO THE SPIRIT OF THE AGE, THE VICTORIANS PREFERRED SELF-HELP OVER POOR RELIEF.

Statistics and surveys were the lifeblood of Victorian social reform, but they did not do much to help the cottager. The problem was a simple one of economics. The agricultural labourer did not earn enough to pay a high rent, and without a reasonable return on their investment, farmers and landowners were reluctant to repair old cottages and build

new ones. Those speculators who bought scraps of land that they packed as densely as they could with the cheapest of all possible hovels, came in for severe criticism. 'Into these wretched habitations (which, even if they adjoin the country, have some of the worst features of town residences) crowd the agricultural labourers of England,' lamented Sir John Simon. But apart from half-hearted attempts at producing some enabling legislation (from 1845, for example, government loans were available under a scheme 'to facilitate estate improvement'), the Victorians, true to the spirit of their age, preferred to rely on self-help and individual initiative rather than on state intervention.

'Providence,' wrote the architect George Gilbert Scott in 1857, 'has ordained the different orders and gradations into which the human family is divided, and it is right and necessary that it should be maintained . . . Wealth must always bring its responsibilities, but a landed proprietor is especially in a responsible position.' The best private cottage-building schemes came from landed proprietors who were shamed, perhaps, by the succession of government reports condemning rural housing conditions. Just as importantly, the more pathologically earnest of them were filled with a sense of *noblesse oblige* and, in response to a newly enfranchised middle class that would not tolerate arrogance and aristocratic hauteur, fired with a deeply felt need to legitimize their privileged position by outward expressions of social responsibility. Or, as a horrified Sir Harry Verney of Claydon put it in 1869 when he discovered the terrible state of cottages in a village close by his Buckinghamshire estate, 'Owners of landed property . . . are not justified in receiving the produce or profits of the land without providing that those whose labour brings the profits are properly and decently cared for.'

Landowners could take their lead from the top. Prince Albert himself (in collaboration with Henry Roberts, architect to a charity with the quintessentially Victorian name of The Society for Improving the Condition of the Labouring Classes) designed a group of four cottages for the Great Exhibition. They were built as a single block – two on the ground floor and two more above – with a deeply recessed two-storey porch crowned by an incongruous Elizabethan parapet providing access to each dwelling. Each cottage comprised a living room, a scullery and privy and three bedrooms. By the mid-nineteenth century these were held to be the minimum requirements for a labouring family. For decency's sake it was essential to have separate bedrooms for parents, sons and daughters. However, as we have seen, the reality was that many still lived in cottages that fell far short of the ideal. In 1867, for example, the Parish Union of Swaffham in Lincolnshire contained 2,051 cottages; sixty-two per cent had two bedrooms, twenty-three per cent had one, and only fifteen per cent could boast of three.

Foremost among the owners of great estates who were prepared to shoulder the rich man's burden were the Dukes of Bedford, whose name was a byword for advanced thinking on the provision of labourers' cottages. The Bedfords' Woburn estate contained a whole village devoted to servicing the building needs of the tenantry. Housing, which was standardized so that doors and windows could be mass-produced during the winter in preparation for new works the following spring, was spartan, 'very plain indeed, but not ugly', in the words of one contemporary. 'The walls inside are whitened brick, not plastered and the whole is very plain but substantial and well finished. The inhabitants seemed enchanted with them and very dirty people became neat and clean in them.' Each cottage consisted of two ground-floor rooms, one with a copper, and two or three bedrooms upstairs. They were built in rows with communal ovens, and ornament was restricted to a concrete slab with a ducal crest. Rents were either a shilling or eighteen pence a week, depending on the number of bedrooms.

Other landowners agreed with the Dukes of Bedford about the need to act responsibly over estate housing. But often their building activity was either an extension of the twin goals of the Victorian landowner – a new country house to improve his physical comfort and a new church for things spiritual – or a disguise for a thoroughly Georgian desire to keep estate workers out of sight, if not out of mind. Between 1838 and 1842, for example, the sixth Duke of Devonshire swept away the village of Edensor in Derbyshire because it was too close to Chatsworth, and after a visit to Blaise Hamlet, decided to rebuild it as a picturesque composition with help from Joseph Paxton (his gardener at the time) and Henry Robertson, a contributor to Loudon's *Encyclopaedia of Cottage, Farm and Villa Architecture*. The new settlement was conceived in an alarming mixture of styles that epitomizes early Victorian eclecticism, 'a perfect compendium of all the prettiest styles of cottage architecture', as one commentator described the village in 1842. 'Everything tends to show his Grace's taste, good feeling, and liberal disposition towards those in humble circumstances', enthused another. Good feeling and liberal disposition, maybe, but one staggers at the combination of Swiss, Norman, castellated Gothic, Tudor, Jacobean and Italianate. 'Taste' is not the word that comes to mind.

Still, the design of most new estate housing was often left to the whims of local builders rather than architects, except in the case of lodges and gatehouses, which were essentially adjuncts to the country house, and, as such, in the domain of the architect. The tension between the cottage as dwelling and the cottage as picturesque object – Woburn versus Blaise Hamlet – persisted throughout the nineteenth century. 'Teach me how to house the poor as an example to others and not as a rich man's fancy', implored the ninth Duke of Bedford in an 1885 letter to Sir Henry Acland, another pioneer in the field of cheap, functional worker-housing for the agricultural labourer.

Rich men's fancies – elaborate Gothic or Elizabethan or Italianate fantasies with finials and towers (and an earth closet) to complement the owner's new eighty-room mansion by Teulon or Salvin – continued to be built, but the second half of the nineteenth century saw a revolution in architects' attitudes towards the cottage. The design of a humble cottage was too serious a business to be left to local builders, who were all too likely to come up with 'spontaneous productions . . . where no external influence is brought to bear upon them', as George Gilbert Scott pointed out in *Secular and Domestic Architecture*. 'Can anything be more at variance with what one would think should be the character of a country village?'

THE ONLY COTTAGE THAT REMAINS FROM THE OLD EDENSOR IN DERBYSHIRE . THE REST OF THE VILLAGE WAS REBUILT BY THE DUKE OF DEVONSHIRE .

Ironically, Scott's own essays in estate cottage design were serious, solemn and rather dull in an earnest, Gothic sort of way. But the point he made was a valid one. Builders on tight budgets with access to railway-borne brick and tile would tend to produce a utilitarian box – a vast improvement on what it replaced, maybe, but something that took no account of vernacular tradition or architectural context. On the other hand, few early Victorian architects took account of tradition or context.

A BLAISE HAMLET-INSPIRED VILLAGE AT SOMERLEYTON, SUFFOLK, BUILT *c*.1850 FOR SIR NORTON PETO.

One of the first to do so was George Devey (1820-86). Little is known of Devey's early life. His uncle was Augustus Egg, the successful genre painter, and his grandfather was an equally successful gunsmith. As a teenager in the late 1830s George spent several years studying in Norwich with the landscape artist John Sell Cotman, whose love of the countryside, sense of composition and eye for topographical detail were invaluable to the young man, especially when he embarked on his career as an architect.

Devey came to Penshurst in Kent in 1850 to work for Sir Philip Sidney, fourth Baron de l'Isle and Dudley, restoring Sidney's romantic medieval home and repairing and adding to a group of fifteenth-century cottages that stood in Leicester Square, close by the old churchyard. Over the next ten years his work there showed that he owed allegiance to the Picturesque *cottage ornée* tradition rather than to the common-sense functionalism favoured by the Dukes of Bedford. But instead of producing parodies of the country cottage, as Nash had done at Blaise, Devey responded to the vernacular traditions of the neighbourhood tactfully and with a cheerful, easy-going élan. Using local techniques and styles – tall chimneys and jettied, timber-framed gables – and a combination of local materials such as roughcast and red brick, tile-hanging and weather-boarding, he created a series of cottages, shops and estate buildings, even a village well, that merged gently with their surroundings. Through it all his goal was to make his buildings appear part of the historic landscape, products of traditional craftsmanship that had grown and mellowed with the centuries. This sentiment was not always appreciated by the locals, if a conversation reported in *Country Life* at the end of the century is anything to go by. Discussing the well, one villager was heard to say to another, 'Might so well have gied us a pump, mightn't he?' To which his companion replied, 'Lord love ye, that wouldn't have been quaint fashioned enough.'

'Quaint fashioned' the Penshurst cottages may be, but they are also peculiarly attractive, an understated antidote to the squalor of rural life in open villages on the one hand, and the solemn excesses of the Gothic Revival on the other. Devey's reputation soon spread, and commissions arrived for estate buildings at Benenden, Fordcombe, Hawkhurst, Nonnington, Leigh, and a host of other Kentish villages. At the same time, he established a thriving country house practice, often combining the building of a mansion with new worker-housing. At Nonnington, halfway between Dover and Canterbury, St Alban's Court (1875-8) is of Tudoresque red brick, with lower courses of ragstone that creep so far and so eccentrically up the walls that the house seems to have evolved over the centuries. Devey's cottages on the estate, with their tall chimneys and plastered, tile-hung and brickwork walls, evoke the same feeling. At Betteshanger near Deal, the transformation of a rambling country house with medieval, Elizabethan, Stuart and Georgian elements into an even more rambling and infinitely more attractive Victorian gentleman's residence was accompanied by the building of some splendid cottages, lodges and a cottage hospital.

Devey's love affair with the Kentish vernacular marks a turning point in attitudes towards cottage design. The next generation of architects, led by Richard Norman Shaw and William Eden Nesfield, journeyed out of London to study Devey's work. More importantly, they ventured into the villages of Kent and Sussex to sketch the yeomen farms, early country houses and tumbledown labourers' homes that had inspired it. On a single August day in 1862, for example, Shaw drew Devey's Penshurst cottages, Penshurst Place itself and two old tile-hung cottages at Bidborough and Tunbridge Wells.

The immediate results of this new interest were the great country houses of the Old English movement, mansions like Shaw's Cragside in Northumberland, that turned their backs on the pedantic historicism of the High Victorians to borrow freely from

A COTTAGE IN BETHERSDEN, KENT, IS A MODEL OF THE OLD KENTISH
STYLE THAT ARCHITECTS LIKE GEORGE DEVEY STROVE TO EMULATE.

different vernacular styles. A side effect of the movement was the legitimization of the seventeenth- and eighteenth-century labourer's cottage as a fit subject for the architect to consider, and not merely as a model or a source of inspiration.

In 1888, a precocious teenaged Edwin Lutyens solemnly explained his principles of architecture to Shaw, by this time one of the most eminent architects of his day, 'that anything that was put up by man should harmonize with what Nature, who had been there first, should dictate. Materials should be drawn from those obtainable in the area and foreign elements strictly eliminated'. A few years later Lutyens was accompanying Gertrude Jekyll on voyages of discovery through Surrey and Sussex. 'Old houses, farms and cottages were searched for,' he later recalled, 'their modest methods of construction discussed, their inmates and the industries that supported them.' Lutyens' design for The Hut at Munstead followed in 1894-5, a careful recreation of a Surrey cottage where Jekyll could entertain guests and live the simple life with only one servant. As is so often the case with the best Domestic Revival architecture, Munstead Wood Hut evoked the past far better than the real thing, and Jekyll used it as an illustration of an old cottage garden in her book *Old West Surrey* (1904).

Most of the other great names in late Victorian architecture also went in for cottages in a romantic vernacular style, both as retreats for wealthy clients and as homes for estate labourers. Nesfield designed a number of Old English cottages in the mid-1860s for the Crewe Hall estate in Cheshire, and Philip Webb produced designs for a pair of semi-detached cottages at Standen, where he was creating a new and very vernacular country house for the lawyer J. S. Beale in the 1890s. Ernest Newton, who worked in Shaw's office

from 1873 to 1879, was adept at mixing styles and materials, as his bailliff's cottage at West Stratton (1880) demonstrates, with its lower walls of brick and flint and jettied upper storey of oak and plaster. Newton also produced designs for an attractive group of seven cottages at the Lever work-colony of Port Sunlight in Cheshire in 1897. Surrounded by neat gardens and low, clipped box hedges, they bring the country cottage into the garden suburb, while their stone, brick and tile construction, the dormers and the roofs' long, sweeping pitch reminds the observer of their vernacular roots.

The impact on cottage design of the Domestic Revival architects was perhaps strongest in the early years of the twentieth century, and detailed consideration of their work properly belongs to the next chapter. But the ground rules were laid down in the nineteenth. W. R. Lethaby summed them up in his memoir of Webb:

Architecture to Webb was first of all a common tradition of honest building. The great architectures of the past had been noble customary ways of building, naturally developed by the craftsmen engaged in the actual works. Building is a folk art. And all art to Webb meant folk expression embodied and expanding in the several mediums of different materials . . . In a word, architecture is building traditionally.

To the architects of the Domestic Revival, 'a common tradition of honest building' meant discarding historical styles in favour of more organic local traditions, building in harmony with the landscape rather than imposing one's will on it. Old country cottages, rambling and asymmetrical with hipped roofs and roughly rendered walls, somehow had more integrity than a Gothic *cottage ornée* or an Italianate villa. The link with the rural buildings of the seventeenth and early eighteenth centuries had the added bonus for young architects of representing a break with the styles of the 1850s and 1860s. More importantly, 'honest building' broke with the mechanistic and utilitarian ideals of modern

COTTAGES AT PORT
SUNLIGHT IN CHESHIRE,
DESIGNED BY ERNEST
NEWTON, 1897.

When one sees climbing plants or any of the shrubs that are so often used as climbers, planted in the usual way on a house or wall, about four feet apart and with no attempt at arrangement, it gives one that feeling of regret for opportunities lost or misused which is the sentiment most often aroused in the mind of the garden critic in the great number of pleasure-grounds that are planted without thought or discernment. Not infrequently in passing along a country road, with eye alert to note the beauties that are so often presented by little wayside cottage gardens, something is seen that may well serve as a lesson in better planting. The lesson is generally one that teaches greater simplicity – the doing of one thing at a time; the avoidance of overmuch detail. One such cottage has under the parlour window an old bush of *Pyrus japonica*. It had been kept well spurred back and must have been a mass of gorgeous bloom in early spring. The rest of the cottage was embowered in an old Grape Vine, perhaps of all wall plants the most beautiful, and, I always think, the most harmonious with cottages or small houses of the cottage class.

It is, like all other matters of garden planning, a question of knowledge and good taste. The kind of wall or house and its neighbouring forms are taken into account and a careful choice is made of the most suitable plants. For my own part I like to give a house, whatever its size or syle, some dominant note in wall-planting. In my own home, which is a house of the large cottage class, the prevailing wall-growths are vines and figs in the south and west, and in a shady northward facing court

between two projecting wings, *Clematis montana* on the two cooler sides, and again a vine upon the other. At one angle on the warmer side of the house, where the height to the eaves is not great, China roses have been trained up, and rosemary, which clothes the whole foot of the wall, is here encouraged to rise with them. The colour of the China rose bloom and the dusky green of rosemary are always to me one of the most charming combinations. In remembrance of the cottage example lately quoted there is *Pyrus japonica* under the long sitting-room window.

I remember another cottage that had a porch covered with the golden balls of *Kerria japonica*, and China roses reaching up the greater part of the low walls of half timber and plastering; the pink roses seeming to ask one which of them were the loveliest in colour; whether it was those that came against the silver-grey of the old oak or those that rested on the warm-white plaster. It should be remembered that of all roses the pink China is the one that is more constantly in bloom than any other, for its first flowers are perfected before the end of May, and in sheltered places the later ones last till Christmas.

The *Clematis montana* in the court riots over the wall facing east and up over the edge of the roof. At least it appears to riot, but is really trained and regulated; the training favouring its natural way of throwing down streamers and garlands of its long bloom-laden cordage. At one point it runs through and over a Guelder Rose that is its only wall companion. Then it turns to the left and is trained in garlands along a moulded oak beam that forms the base of a timbered wall with plastered panels.

Another of these Clematises, which, like the montana of gardens, is very near the wild species and is good for all the same purposes, is *C. Flammula*, blooming in September. Very slightly trained it takes the form of flowery clouds . . . I do not think there is any incident in my garden that has been more favourably noticed than the happy growth of these two plants together. The wall faces north a little west, and every year it is a delight to see not only the beauty of associated form, but the loveliness of the colouring; for the Clematis bloom has the warm white of foam and the Spiraea has leaves of the rather pale green of Lady Fern, besides a graceful fern-like form and slight twist or turn also of a fern-like character. But this Clematis has many other uses, for bowers, arches and pergolas, as well as for many varied aspects of wild gardening.

There is no lovelier or purer blue than that of the newly opened *Ipomea rubro-coerulea*, popularly known as Heavenly Blue and well deserving the name. It must be raised in heat early in the year and be put out in June against a warm wall. Here it is in a narrow border at the foot of a wall facing southwest, where, by the aid of a few short pea-sticks, it climbs into the lower branches of a vine. The vine is one of the Chasselas kind, with leaves of a rather pale green, almost yellowish-green col-ouring that makes the best possible foil to the pure blue of the Ipomea. To my eye it is the most enjoyable colour-feast of the year. *Solanum crispum*, with purple flowers in goodly bunches, is one of the best of wall shrubs.

Another of the tender plants that is beautiful for walls and for free rambling over other wall-growths is *Solanum jasminoides*. Its white clusters come into bloom in middle summer and persist till latest autumn. In two gardens near me it is of singular beauty; in the one case on the sunny wall of a sheltered court where it covers a considerable space, in the other against a high south retaining-wall where, from the terrace above, the flowers are seen against the misty woodland of the middle distance and the pure grey-blue of the faraway hills. Turning round on the very same spot, there is the remarkable growth of the Sweet Verbena, that owes its luxuriance to its roots and main shoots being under shelter. There must be unending opportunities, where there are verandahs, of having just such bowers of sweetness to brush against in passing and to waft scented air to the windows of the rooms above.

GERTRUDE JEKYLL, *COLOUR SCHEMES FOR THE FLOWER GARDEN*, 1908.

COTTAGE DESIGNS

FROM *STUDIO YEAR*

BOOK, 1912.

industrial society, everything that progressive late Victorians most despised. The overall impact on rural housing may have been – indeed, was – marginal, but the movement brought the modern cottage as art object into the public domain as effectively as the pictures of Helen Allingham and her 'sunny England'.

The constant, grinding poverty of cottage-dwellers depicted by so many Victorian official reports and investigations only tell one side of the story of cottage life. They tend to focus on the worst cases, just as the idealized visions of rural paradise painted by Allingham, Birket Foster and their fellow-artists represent the best. Most nineteenth-century cottage-dwellers may have been quicker to recognize the realism than the romance, but daily life still rested somewhere in between.

This reality is reflected in the various informal mechanisms for helping cottage-dwellers that existed alongside parish relief and the workhouse. One response was voluntary charity, and this remained an important element in rural life throughout the nineteenth century. The union activist Joseph Arch, born in 1826 in a 'homely cottage' in the village of Barford in Warwickshire, recalled how in his childhood soup, coal and other items were dispensed regularly from the rectory to 'nearly every poor person in the village'. 'Nearly', because the Arch family was excluded from this largesse after Joseph's mother fell out with the parson's wife, 'a kind of would-be lady pope', over the latter's decree that all girls attending the local school should have their hair cut round like a basin; Mrs Arch refused to have her two daughters looking like 'prison girls'. In general, however, most cottagers were not as proud as Mrs Arch, and voluntary charity was a handy tool for reinforcing deference and hierarchy within the village community.

It also provided much-needed relief in times of high prices and high rural unemployment. By the mid-nineteenth century the aristocracy was devoting between four and seven per cent of their gross income to charitable purposes, and the contributions ranged far beyond doles of soup and coal, encompassing church-building, pensions to retired employees, subscriptions to schools and even regular payments to village cricket clubs. Lower down the social scale, the charity books that were kept from 1868 to 1893 by the Le Stranges, gentry landowners in Norfolk, shows how the £5 or so a year that they spent was distributed. Gifts of beer, broth, mutton and tea were given to poor families, to the

RURAL LIFE PRESERVED: IN THE 1880S, MISS HERSCHEL OF LITTLEMORE, OXFORDSHIRE,

RECORDED HER OWN VILLAGE IN WATERCOLOUR.

elderly, to widows and to the sick, often in the course of personal visits to their cottages.

Aid to the impoverished cottager came in a variety of other forms, many of which are well nigh impossible to quantify. There were village-based friendship societies and benefit clubs, although these often came and went with alarming frequency as a small capital base or simple financial mismanagement led them to collapse. One might borrow from friends when times were hard, or go into debt to the village shop for the next week's wages – a system known as 'one week under another'. If this would not suffice, the storekeeper would extend further credit, up to £5 or £10 in some cases, on the understanding that a portion of the debt was paid off each week, and that at harvest-time (when there was extra work available) or when the family pig was slaughtered, a larger sum would be handed over against the debt.

The rescue network for those at the bottom end of the earnings scale, and for those who had fallen off it altogether, was informal and diverse. For those in work, for example, we can arrive at fairly accurate estimates of rural wages in Victorian times, but it is much harder to know the extent to which these earnings were supplemented. Cottages were sometimes provided free of rent or let at a low rate. Most farmworkers had a daily allowance of beer or cider at least until 1887, when the Truck Act of that year barred the practice, and in some areas, where workers refused to accept the change, for much longer.

PROVIDING RECREATION. THE BILLIARD ROOM FOR VILLAGERS ON LORD
HARROWBY'S STAFFORDSHIRE ESTATE , BUILT BY E. GUY DAWBER, *c.* 1905.

Fuel, bags of flour, milk, cheese, bacon and other produce were often provided as payment in kind or at below market rates, in addition to wages.

There was also still a certain amount of self-sufficiency, in spite of the fact that the traditional combination of casual wage-labour and husbandry had been dealt a hard blow by eighteenth-century enclosures. Many cottagers kept a pig and grew their own vegetables. Well into the twentieth century two-up, two-down cottages were still being built in Somerset complete with brick pigstys and quarter-acre strips of garden that were put down almost exclusively to potatoes and other vegetables. No doubt a certain amount of bartering went on as well. In 1838 William Howitt recalled how during a tour of Lancashire and Yorkshire he had met a smallholder who 'was never known to part with money except to the tax-gatherer'. This man cut peat on the fells all summer long, and when he needed to repair his cart, he bargained with the local wheelwright or blacksmith to pay them in peat. He baked his own oatcake, and paid the miller in peat for grinding his oats. He drank milk from his own cow and made his own clogs with wood cut from his own alder.

Most cottagers, then, managed to get by, if only just, and it is a source of amazement that farmworkers in general were longer-lived by far than their urban counterparts. An 1850 survey of life expectancy among twenty-five occupational groups showed that

HEALTH AND EFFICIENCY – THE GYMNASIUM IN THE VILLAGE CLUB AT
SANDON, LORD HARROWBY'S ESTATE.

the rural labourer came close to the top of the league. At age twenty he could expect to live for another forty-five years, and only carpenters were able to improve on that.

It is tempting to think that plain, wholesome food and a healthy outdoor existence were responsible for extended life expectancy. However, a long life was not necessarily a healthy one, as Canon Girdlestone pointed out, 'The labourer . . . is long lived, but in the prime of life "crippled up", i.e. disabled with rheumatism, . . . poor living and sour cider.' Even allowing for regional variations – in the prosperous northern counties milk, potatoes and meat formed a more significant part of the rural family's diet than they did in the south, for example – meals were often frugal. An 1863 enquiry into the diets of 'the poorer labouring classes' showed that bread was still the staple, with an average of $1\frac{1}{2}$ lbs being consumed by each person each day. Potatoes came next, and meat was a rarity. Thirty per cent of the 509 families who took part in the enquiry reported that they never ate butcher's meat. But food was not distributed equally within the family, as menus collected for the survey demonstrate:

Breakfast – milk gruel, or bread and water, or tea and bread. Dinner – meat for husband only; others vegetables only. Tea and supper – bread or potatoes.

Breakfast – husband, milk and bread; family, tea, bread and butter. Dinner – husband, bacon daily; others, three days

MOST VICTORIAN COTTAGERS RELIED HEAVILY ON THE PRODUCE FROM THEIR OWN GARDENS FOR FOOD.

weekly, potatoes or bread, tea. Tea – tea, bread and butter.

Although his wife and children may also be employed in casual work in the fields, it was generally held that the man of the house should receive the greater share of the food, since his work was the hardest. 'It is remarkable,' said the authors of the report, 'that this is not only acquiesced in by the wife, but felt by her to be right, and even necessary for the maintenance of the family.'

The cottager's diet tended to improve during the later years of the nineteenth century. At the beginning of the 1900s an old labourer told Rider Haggard how during the Crimean War, when bread cost a shilling a loaf on a weekly wage of eight or nine shillings, he existed for months at a time on bread and onions, washed down with small beer. He and his wife could not afford tea, but she 'imitated the appearance of that beverage' by soaking a burnt crust of bread in boiling water. 'Things is better now', the labourer said, and so they were for much of the rural population. With wages rising and food prices

INCREASINGLY CRAMPED CONDITIONS IN RURAL COTTAGES WAS BELIEVED
TO AID THE SPREAD OF TYPHUS IN THE 19TH CENTURY.

COTTAGE RANGE FROM THE
CATALOGUE OF BARNARD,
BISHOP AND BARNARD,
NOVEMBER, 1881.

falling as a result of the agricultural depression of the 1870s and 1880s, many labourers were materially better off at the end of Victoria's reign than their grandparents had been at the beginning. A Devon farmer in the 1880s described the change in his own neighbourhood over the previous generation:

The peasant certainly lives very much better than his father did. Living, during the last generation, consisted chiefly of barley bread and broth for breakfast, with a little skimmed 'country' cheese. For dinner he had barley dumpling with a very small piece of bacon in the middle – and barley bread, with a little salt fish or bacon for his supper. But when potatoes were good, plentiful, and cheap, this diet was often varied by large quantities of potatoes being used . . . If the peasant then tasted meat, it was generally bacon – beef or mutton being, as a rule, a treat. Wheat was sometimes mixed with the barley to make loaves, and the peasant's wife then always made and baked the family bread at home under an iron kettle on the hearth . . . But the peasant eats very little, if any, barley now. His wife generally buys wheaten bread, ready made, and baked by the small town or village baker, who delivers it at the labourers' doors; and most rural districts have their butchers, who deliver meat in the same way.

With these improvements came other changes in the cottager's daily life as, through better communications and the efforts of reformers and philanthropists, the gulf between rural and urban culture began to diminish. By the 1880s the traditional smock frock of the agricultural worker in the south-west was almost a thing of the past, replaced by cloth jackets. Village clothing clubs, usually presided over by the vicar's wife, encouraged a woman to subscribe a few pence a week. At the end of each year her savings would be returned to her, perhaps with a little extra donated by the squire or from parish funds. But the cottager's wife was not to be trusted with money, so her return came in the form of a ticket to take to the draper's, and her purchases often had to be approved by the fundholder. 'This rule serves as a precaution against the money being expended on light, useless finery.'

This desire for social control pervaded much middle-class thinking about the cottager's moral and social welfare in Victorian times. Respectability – which in practice meant conforming to prevailing bourgeois convention – was all, and traditional village pastimes, for example, were not respectable. But old cultures and old beliefs lingered. Francis Kilvert

THE TRADITIONAL LABOURER'S SMOCK HAD BECOME A RARITY BY THE END OF THE 19TH CENTURY.

was told in 1871 that the frog-woman of Presteigne in Powys, who used to hop from her cottage to chapel and back, behaved as she did because she had been cursed in her mother's womb. Ancient cures for such ailments as whooping cough – giving the sufferer a roast mouse to eat, for example, or putting the head of a live trout into their mouth – were still practised. And even in the early years of the twentieth century, it was claimed in Devon that a deformed child could be cured by passing it three times through the cleft in a split ash tree at dawn. This particular custom, described at Selborne by Gilbert White in 1776, was said to be 'derived down from our Saxon ancestors, who practised it before their conversion to Christianity'.

The old festivals and pastimes, the Whitsuntide processions and May-Day revels and harvest feasts and village fairs, also lingered, but they came under increasing attack for their immorality and vulgarity. Alfred Williams, looking back with regret in the years before the First World War at changes in the villages of the Upper Thames, described the process of decline:

'THERE IS A VULGARITY IN
MOST POPULAR CUSTOMS
THAT OFFENDS INVARIABLY
OUR PRESENT TASTES.'

The sight of so many 'poor foolish' peasant folk thronging the streets . . . was an offence to those who affected a superiority of taste and were possessed with means of indulging it. They did not like the noise of the crowd; they said it was hateful and abominable, pure barbarism; it was time it was put a stop to; they could see all manner of evil in it, it was nothing but a 'drunken, rowdy show', a public pest, and a nuisance. So, in time, from one cause and another, the old sports fell away; this was prohibited, and that was prohibited; a standing was refused here, and something else objected to there . . . The old sports and festivals used to brighten up the year for farm-people, and if they were rude and simple, noisy and boisterous, they served their purpose very well, and were always hailed with unfeigned joy and delight.

Rational recreation would, it was hoped, take the place of the drunkenness, casual sex and brawling that were seen as the inevitable consequences of village festivities. 'The more our humble classes come to taste of the pleasures of books and the intellect, and the deep fireside affections which grow out of the growth of heart and mind,' wrote William Howitt with touching innocence in 1838, 'the less charms will the outward forms of rejoicing have for them . . . there is a vulgarity in most popular customs that offends invariably our present tastes.' So public lectures, lantern shows and outings were arranged, often by the nonconformist churches, who had considerable success in providing alternative recreations that would both attract new members and keep old ones out of the ale-house. That ale-house was the chapel's main rival for the cottager's leisure time. It remained the chief social centre and meeting place in most rural communities, for men at least – their wives rarely set foot inside the door. The local public house, said Richard Jeffries, was often 'the only place of amusement to which [the agricultural labourer] can resort'. It was here that he met with his friends and neighbours

VILLAGE FESTIVALS LIKE THE MAY-DAY REVELS WERE REGARDED WITH

SUSPICION AND DISTASTE BY MANY VICTORIAN REFORMERS.

to gossip, drink and play a game of quoits, skittles or dominoes. Here he also learned the news of the day, by either reading the papers and journals that many inns began to provide during the later nineteenth century or, if he could not read, having them read to him.

It is not surprising that other traditional forms of recreation had all but died out by the beginning of the twentieth century. There was much more contact with the 'civilizing' influence of urban life. Every cottager in every village would know someone who had moved into the towns in search of work, and a spreading rail network (by 1898 there were 15,000 miles of line open in England alone) meant that isolated and self-contained rural communities were almost a thing of the past, except in the most remote outlying areas. A younger, better-educated generation tended to look askance at the folk-customs and traditions of the past. Landlords, imbued with a moral fire and a keen sense of their duty to ensure their tenants conformed to prevailing middle-class values, were quick to enforce those values by all the means at their disposal.

This notion of careful social control is perfectly illustrated in F. G. Heath's 1880 account of the model village of Wilcot, some eight miles east of Devizes in Wiltshire. A mixture of brick and stone, thatch and slate, the fifty or so 'pretty cottages' that made up Victorian Wilcot all had good-sized lattice windows, two or three bedrooms, a sitting room and a kitchen. Most had attractive gardens, with fruit, vegetables and flowers, so that 'over all there is an air of brightness and freshness, and there is especially an absence of the sort of "soiled" appearance which too frequently is noticeable in workmen's dwellings'. Rents were no higher than a shilling a week, plus eightpence a year for a contract chimney-sweep, who came twice annually. Wilcot was a closed village in that all the cottages belonged to one landlord. No lodgers were allowed, and families were moved around from house to house as children were born, grew and left home, to make the best use of accommodation.

The key that allowed entry to this Stepford village was, as Heath makes clear, a high moral tone among its inmates:

THE ALE HOUSE, THE CHIEF SOCIAL CENTRE AND MEETING PLACE IN MOST RURAL COMMUNITIES.

A WILTSHIRE VILLAGE AT THE TURN OF THE CENTURY. VICTORIAN LANDLORDS WERE

EAGER TO STAMP OUT TRADITIONAL FORMS OF RECREATION.

If any member of a family occupying a Wilcot cottage is known to be 'drunk' notice to quit is forthwith served upon that individual. Similarly, if the daughter of a labourer proves to be 'unfortunate' on returning from service or otherwise, the family to which she belongs are also required – on the circumstances becoming known – to leave the house they occupy.

There was only one public house, and that was closed on Sundays, not because the villagers' landlord forbade it, says Heath with a breathtakingly naive leap of the credibility gap, but 'because there is no demand for Sunday trade on the part of the inhabitants'. The weekends were sober and steady affairs, in contrast to the neighbouring village of Oare, where there were plenty of pubs and where seldom a Saturday night passed without a fight in the street. 'Surely,' says Heath, 'this simple statement speaks volumes for the moral effect of a decent dwelling, and of the thoughtful and constant supervision of an excellent landlord.'

Indeed it does.

CHAPTER VI

Looking for a New England

1900-1950

*During the past few years the country-cottage mania has assumed an alto-
gether virulent form . . . For instance, it is difficult to find within a forty-
mile radius of Charing Cross any really dilapidated farm-house, lean-to, or
rustic dwelling which is not inhabited during the pleasanter months of the
year by persons for whom it was most assuredly not built . . . In other words,
the aristocracy and the plutocracy haunt these places, in spite of their cheapness, in spite of their meanness, in spite of their plain lack of drainage – and
in spite of the obvious fact that there is no room in them. And of course the
middle classes, upper and lower, follow suit, having nothing else to do.*

T. W. H. CROSLAND, *THE COUNTRY LIFE*, 1906

For those who succumbed to Crosland's 'country-cottage mania', Eunice, whose column on 'Home Decoration' was a regular feature of *The Lady* in the 1890s, had plenty of ideas for turning a humble rural retreat into the House Beautiful. Turquoise paper, ivory paint and a Burmese carpet were just the thing for the cottage parlour, with curtains of floral-patterned cretonne in summer and gold serge in winter, a valance of orange silk for the mantelpiece and a bamboo lamp-table. A small centre table with four rush-bottomed chairs, two wicker easy chairs with silk pillows and cretonne cushions and a low divan in the window will complete the room.

The main bedroom, which 'will want careful furnishing, to make it look nice, and yet give sufficient space for the swinging of the proverbial pussy', might be decorated with a pink floral paper on a cream ground, with green painted woodwork. Matting would do for the floor, and the bed, of plain iron enamelled white, should have a deep frill of pink and white brocade nailed to the wall behind the head and a bedspread to match. To finish off the room you would need a combination chest of drawers, wash-stand, toilet-table and mirror (price: £4.2s.6d.), a corner wardrobe at 28s., with pale green serge curtains and a light wood pediment, and curtains and side frills of pink and white cretonne.

The second bedroom is turned into a dressing room, decorated in yellow, green and white. The hall has a floor-covering of black-and-white linoleum and the staircase is decked out with terracotta wallpaper and stair-carpet. Two drainpipes, painted sealing-wax red, serve as stands for umbrellas and walking sticks. The garden, both back and front, 'should be a blaze of flowers in summer'. Eunice recommends phlox, gaillardias, irises, cabbage-roses, sweet peas, sunflowers and dahlias. An ivy-hung trellis keeps the plainly furnished kitchen and scullery hidden from sight.

The aspirations and living conditions of agricultural labourers and their families may have improved quite a lot by the end of the nineteenth century, but this is clearly no ordinary cottage. Few cottagers were in a position to spend two months wages on a dressing table, for one thing. And the idea of devoting the whole of a cottage garden to cabbage-roses and sweet peas would have seemed like madness to a family that relied on produce from a vegetable patch to supplement their diet.

But *The Lady*'s simple cottage is not intended for the rural worker and his family. It is, in fact, a sanctuary from the cares of urban life for the young, middle-class couple who wanted to get away from it all in the country without the problems of hunting for lodgings or the 'fear of infection from previous occupants'. This place in the country could be theirs for only 4s.6d. a week, and in all likelihood a local woman could be found to live in as caretaker in return for the rent-free use of a third bedroom and the kitchen. 'I recommend my idea,' says Eunice, 'to young wives who see their husbands growing pale from the daily routine of a City office, and who will drink in health with every breath of country air – a luxury easily obtained by taking "week-end" trips to the cottage.'

As the twentieth century dawned, the Victorian dream of an unspoilt England of leafy country lanes, rambling manor houses, and pretty villages filled with picturesque thatched cottages, held a powerful appeal for the city-dweller. The town was noisy and dirty. Only the countryside could provide 'those fair, far, still places' that offered 'the beauty . . . the quiet which the city does not, cannot give', in the words of Octavia Hill, the

GLORIFYING TRADITIONAL ACCESSORIES, *THE LADY*'S EUNICE

RECOMMENDED A VALANCE OF ORANGE SILK FOR THE MANTELPIECE.

housing reformer and founder of the National Trust. The town was morally bankrupt, the home of greed and vulgarity; it is no coincidence that the spiritual if rather fey Schlegel sisters are perfectly at home in the rural landscape of E. M. Forster's *Howard's End* (1910), while the philistine Wilcoxes are constantly being struck down with hay fever. The town was the epitome of rapid and bewildering change, poverty and social unrest. The real England was not to be found there, in the sprawling suburbs, overcrowded tenements and bustling thoroughfares of the major cities. It was to be found in the lanes and villages of Surrey, Kent and the Cotswolds, where the old social order under squire and parson still existed, where traditional values still remained securely in place.

This old England was of course a new England, a rose-tinted artificial construct born of dissatisfaction with the humdrum realities of industrial life. But that did not lessen its attraction, and during the Edwardian period – indeed, far beyond it – the steady flow of country-dwellers into the cities passed a stream of townsfolk travelling in the opposite direction. The more idealistic attempted to put William Morris's utopian vision of craft communities into practice, with varying degrees of success. C. R. Ashbee's Guild of Handicrafts, about 150 strong, decamped from London to Chipping Camden in Gloucestershire in 1902. 'Good honest craftmanship,' said Ashbee, 'is better done the

TO THE TOWN-DWELLER, THE COUNTRY COTTAGE PROMISED 'THE BEAUTY, THE QUIET WHICH THE CITY DOES NOT, CANNOT GIVE.'

nearer the people get in touch with the elemental things of life.' The experiment continued for some seven years. At nearby Sapperton, a more enduring project was launched by Ernest Gimson and the Barnsley brothers, who set out to revive traditional furniture-making crafts in an appropriate setting. (It was more lasting in a commercial sense, but on a personal level it was not so successful: Ernest Gimson and Ernest Barnsley quickly fell out, or at least their wives did, and although they continued to live virtually next door to each other, the two families never spoke.) At Whiteway, also in Gloucestershire, an anarchist colony that was set up at the turn of the century scandalized its respectable neighbours by preaching free love alongside communal cultivation of the land. Other, less-advanced country-lovers followed *The Lady*'s advice

THE DOMESTIC REVIVAL: A COTTAGE AT PINBURY PARK,

GLOUCESTERSHIRE, DESIGNED BY SIDNEY BARNSLEY.

and bought or rented a cottage of their own for weekends and summer holidays.

The Edwardian urbanite's obsession with the countryside was shrewdly summed up in Crosland's ascerbic 1907 satire, *The Country Life*: 'Broadly, and for the benefit of those who wish to be accurately informed, we may define the country as that portion of England in which one ought most certainly not to live.' He also maintained that villagers, instead of dancing round the maypole on the village green as they should, get drunk and talk about horse-racing. Grocers will only sell you their goods at 'an enhanced price', while the country butcher is 'absolutely incapable of distinguishing between meat that is fit for human consumption and meat that is not'. His salt beef, which the butcher is fond of selling you in place of something he does not have, 'is of a quality and toughness which would

make a mule shudder'. And as for the country cottage that is the pot of gold at the end of so many town-dwellers' rainbows, it is frankly uninhabitable, according to Crosland. There are rats under the floorboards, sixty thousand million black ants behind the wallpaper and enough fungi under the carpet to stock a museum. Ivy grows indoors as well as out of doors, the glass blows out of the windows, there are no drains and 'the well is geographically next door to the cesspool, though a floor or so below it'. And yet, says Crosland, people will go and live in cottages.

So they did. Paradoxically, this influx of middle-class weekenders (and commuters, especially in the southeast where rail links provided fast and regular access to London) meant that the semi-feudal social order that was such an integral part of the appeal of rural life for urbanites was steadily eroded by their presence. With the zeal of the new convert they often threw themselves wholeheartedly into village life. The men drank in the local pub, the women took an active role in church activities. But they simply did not fit into the established social structure with its hierarchies, its deference and its network of economic interdependence.

THE COUNTRY 'COTTAGE', THE POT OF GOLD AT THE END OF THE TOWN-DWELLER'S RAINBOW.

The rural landscape was good because it was not new, because however falsely, it appeared to embody all the precious values that modern urban society had lost – stability and innocence, continuity and calm, a deep-rooted connection with the forces of nature. The old country cottage served as a convenient emblem for those values, and throughout the early

The Cottage Homes of England
HOUGHTON. SUSSEX.

A.R.QUINTON

The Cottage Homes of England
STONELEIGH. WARWICKSHIRE.

A.R.QUINTON

The Cottage Homes of England
EAST HENDRED. BERKS.

A.R.QUINTON

1900s a steady spate of books on the subject appeared, all looking fondly back at a mythical rural past and all aimed at an essentially urban middle-class readership who browsed through the lithographs and photos, dreaming that one day such a quaint old cottage might be theirs. The publisher Batsford, for example, produced a successful 'Old Cottage' series, with titles like *Old Cottages and Farmhouses in the Cotswold District* and *Old Cottages and Farmhouses in Kent and Sussex*.

Stewart Dick, in *The Cottage Homes of England* (1909), with its sixty-four atmospheric Allingham plates, neatly sums up the appeal of the cottage. Chapters with headings like 'Old Farmhouses', 'Old Country Inns', 'Old Gardens', even 'The Old Village Life', conjure up a rosy nostalgia. The mansions of the great are more like museums or picture galleries than homes, says Dick: their icy splendour is unreal and wearisome. The Victorian middle-class house, itself 'a monument of respectable bad taste', has been replaced by the artistic suburban villa, with its cheap over-ornamented furniture, cheap stamped metalwork and art muslin curtains. The clutter of reproductions, photographs and ornaments 'makes one long for the dullness of the Victorian house, which at least had a sort of after-dinner feeling of repose. The other suggests indigestion and a waking nightmare.' It is the cottage that best represents things English, because it conforms to Edwardian ideas of what a home should be, for 'the home and the family circle have always been the real centre of English life'. Authentic England lies in unspoilt villages and hamlets:

RURAL ENGLAND, A ROSE-TINTED, ARTIFICIAL IDEAL, BORN OF A GROWING DISSATISFACTION WITH THE INDUSTRIAL AGE.

Such places have no history at all, their life has not been set in the public eye,
and they have always been so wrapt up in their own affairs, that they have

never noticed how time is passing, and so they have brought down into the life of today the traditions of two or three hundred years ago.

But though they do not pose, those quiet places, yet it is through them that the deep, main current of English life has flowed.

Dick concentrates on the counties popularized by the Arts and Crafts movement – Kent and Surrey, Sussex and Wessex, the Cotswolds. The buildings of the West Midlands came in for their share of attention in *Old Cottages, Farm Houses, and Other Half-Timber Buildings in Shropshire, Herefordshire and Cheshire* (1904). This collection of one hundred photographs taken by the architectural woodworker James Parkinson shows a breathtaking array of timber-framing. There is the close vertical studwork of a pair of cottages at Pembridge in Herefordshire that are built on such a steeply inclined street that flights of steps like mounting blocks rise up from the pavement to their front doors. A selection of simple dormered and gabled Shropshire cottages is also included along with the more familiar splendours of Gawsworth and Little Moreton. The accompanying text is by the architect Edward Ould, something of a specialist in timber-framed buildings. His practice included designs for a series of half-timbered villas and country houses, including Dee Hills in Cheshire for Thomas Hughes, author of *Tom Brown's Schooldays*, and Wightwick Manor near Wolverhampton, for the paint manufacturer Theodore Mander, who fur-

TURN-OF-THE-CENTURY VILLAGE LIFE AT WROXTON NEAR BANBURY.

nished it with items by Morris & Co. In his introduction to *Old Cottages, Farm Houses, and Other Half-Timber Buildings*, Ould recommends the use of timber-framing for modern housing, since 'no style of building will harmonize so quickly and so completely with its surroundings and so soon pass through the crude and brand-new period'.

❧ ❧ ❧

In 1912 *Country Life* ran a competition to design a cottage that could be built for £550. The site given was a long one, lying on a north-south axis and fairly level except for a rise of a few feet towards the northern boundary with the road. There were three judges: *Country Life*'s favourite architect, Edwin Lutyens; Arthur Bolton, another architect and regular contributor to the magazine's series on 'Country Homes'; and Lawrence Weaver, the architectural editor.

Now £550 was quite a large sum in 1912, when an agricultural labourer's weekly wage might range from eighteen shillings to a pound in Northumberland, Cumberland and Durham down to twelve or thirteen shillings in Oxfordshire, Wiltshire and Dorset. But these were no ordinary cottages, and it is an indication of how widely

A TIMBER-FRAMED COTTAGE BUILT FOR THE ARTIST H. H. LA THANGUE IN 1897.

THE INTERIOR OF LATHANGUE'S PERROT COTTAGE. OLD WAS BEST, EVEN IF IT HAD TO BE BUILT TO LOOK THAT WAY.

CHARLES GASCOYNE'S PERSPECTIVE OF C. F. W. DENING'S PRIZE-WINNING

'COTTAGE', COMPLETE WITH TENNIS COURT.

the word was coming to be interpreted that they could be described as 'cottages' at all.

Take, for example, the prize-winning design, which was submitted by C. F. W. Dening. The plans of Dening's £550 cottage show that the northern elevation is almost blind – most of the rooms face south to take advantage of the sun – with a small entrance hall, a living room, dining room, kitchen and other domestic offices (larder, pantry and scullery) on the ground floor, and four decent-sized bedrooms and a bathroom above.

In Charles Gascoyne's perspective, taken from the south, we see a hipped-roofed doll's house set in a formal garden. Two pavilions flank the 'cottage', one is a garden house, the other holds a garage and electricity plant. Beneath a broken pediment a door opens onto a terrace with lily ponds and parterres, and in the foreground two ghostly figures amble across a tennis court enclosed by high hedges and terminating in a curving arbour. To the left there is a long and similarly enclosed bowling green.

Pedimented entrances? Garden pavilions? Tennis courts and bowling greens? This is a long way from Dr Johnson's mean habitation, and just as far from the Edwardian labourer's cottage or the quaint picturesque arcadia of period paintings. The brief, in fact, was for a holiday cottage 'for people who want a country retreat and can afford the expense of keeping up a big garden'. On top of the £550 budget, another £150 was allowed for the garden and a further £100 for the motor-house.

All the entrants in the competition came up with equally grandiose designs. The third prize went to an attractive scheme by Lucas and Lodge for a main block linked to two flanking single-storey pavilions, one containing the garage and the other with stores for coal and gas and a WC for the servants. There are three entrances off the road: one to the motor-house, another to the kitchens and a central pair of gates leading to the front door via a miniature version of a circular carriage drive. Most architects included vernacular details – some weather-boarding here, a huge thatched roof there, inglenooks and pantiles and self-consciously irregular plans. But there are loggias, piazzas and pergolas, servant accommodation and circular parlours – even, in Cyril Farey's second-place design, 'a version of the rural Italian manner, reminiscent of a present phase in American domestic architecture', a columned hall, which earned some sharp words from Lawrence Weaver. 'It would be unwise to put pillars into a hall measuring only six feet in width, in the attempt to suggest a minute Italian cortile.' Clearly the cottage had been redefined in just as dramatic a fashion as the *cottage ornée* of the early nineteenth century. To architects and clients in the golden years before the First World War, a cottage could be anything from a labourer's home all the way up to a house in the country that was not quite a country house.

REDEFINING THE
COTTAGE – A 1913
DESIGN BY C. J. KAY
FOR A HOUSE AT
CLIMPING, SUSSEX

THE THIRD-PRIZE WINNER
BY GEOFFRY LUCAS AND
ARTHUR LODGE IN THE
'COUNTRY LIFE' £600-
COTTAGE AND GARDEN
COMPETI-TION OF 1912.

Many architects were not averse to applying vernacular detail to houses that were much more than weekend retreats. The Leys, Hertfordshire, designed in 1901 by the Scottish architect George Walton for the portrait photographer J. B. B. Wellington is one example. (The commission probably came about as a result of Walton's work in the 1890s on Kodak shops – Wellington was the first manager of Kodak's Harrow works.) Walton uses what was rapidly becoming a conventional Arts and Crafts vocabulary: a hipped roof and a mixture of roughcast, brick and tile, with lattice windows. But behind those lattices there is a centrally placed triple-height living hall, complete with billiard table and Art Nouveau ironwork. Detmar Blow learned his Arts and Crafts theory and his socialism at the feet of Ruskin himself. A chance meeting in Abbeville Cathedral with the aging and periodically mad Ruskin in 1888 had led to his accompanying the sage on an extended tour through France and Italy. Blow's country houses, quiet, lyrical, understated, sought to preserve the Arts and Crafts ideals of honest and unobtrusive craftsmanship, while at the same time creating something quite new (and quite beautiful) out of traditional vernacular and historical elements. Hilles, the house in Gloucestershire that he began to build for himself in

1914 and that remained incomplete at his death in 1939, is grand, certainly – but its simple detailing, its evident joy in the use of natural materials and plain workmanship, are evidence that Blow had learned Ruskin's message well.

Others, too, created something new and exciting from the previous generation's interest in the vernacular. Edward Prior took from it a fanatical devotion to the use of local materials: at Kelling Place in Norfolk (1904-6, now known as Home Place), Prior dug out an acre of land on the site to provide pebbles and sand for building. C. F. A. Voysey, who wanted his buildings 'to play into the hands of nature', demanded that above all the new architecture should be simple:

> *Try the effect of a well-proportioned room, with whitewashed walls, plain carpet and simple oak furniture and nothing in it but necessary articles of use – and one pure ornament in the form of a simple vase of flowers.*

'The cottage is his ideal, even when he is building houses of a size and luxuriousness more appropriate to a palace than a cottage', Hermann Muthesius wrote of Voysey in *Das englische Haus* (1904). The long, low lines of a Voysey house show how far the idea of the cottage had travelled since the mid-nineteenth century.

RUSTIC SIMPLICITY WAS THE IDEAL FOR THE COTTAGE INTERIOR IN THE
EARLY 19TH CENTURY.

HOW TO KNOW BEAUTY IN FURNITURE

The particular significance of people's desire to beautify their houses with architectural furniture is that it is evidence of a certain belief in their own judgement; that it shows in them the coming again of that home-making instinct which has been supposed to be peculiarly British. Certainly up to the middle of the last century this was the case, and the Englishman's home being his castle, he made it as comfortable as he could. His Turkey carpets were the genuine article, and his mahogany table had no need to be screened by a chenille cover because the legs only were of that wood. Horsehair and repp conveyed the impression that permanency was the aim.

In the succeeding generations, it was just this quality that was lacking, and the average home of that day suggested that the owner was a bird of passage who, having bought the effects of a previous migrant, was prepared to pass them on at the shortest notice to a following one. The furniture was deplorably made and very cheap; far too cheap to have been made under fair conditions, and it appeared to be considered an advantage that so soon as it became shabby, which it very speedily did, it was a matter of trifling expense to renew it. Pretty came into use as an adjective, and a more unarchitectural word was never invented. Permanency was not sought. To consider seriously the furnishing of house and home on the basis of the knowledge that the furniture so acquired would have to be lived with for the rest of one's life made the experiment as hazardous as matrimony. Ability to do so reflects an equable and well-trained mind and an amount of knowledge that

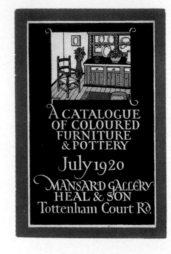

SIMPLICITY IN FURNITURE DESIGN AS ENVISIONED BY HEAL AND SON.

the laymen did not then possess. The connoisseur of the eighteenth century was so appreciative of fine work that he generally managed to obtain it, and one's hope is that in this twentieth century he may blossom into life again . . . [To] have one's house fitted with architectural furniture, shows, at least, that the owner has the faculty of being able to make up his mind, that he knows exactly what he wants, and also that he is making a home that shall in each succeeding year be more a part of himself, rather than the mere furnishing of a house taken for a short period. In the turmoil of the mechanical age he seems to have lived mostly in the pantechnicon vans of the remover . . . and in diverse other ways he pretended that the home and its surroundings was no longer of any consequence, and had, in fact, lost all its significance. Then, like the baby in the tale, he tired of seeing the wheels go round, and felt once more the necessity of a resting-place where peace might be enjoyed after turmoil, and strength gathered for the living of his arduous life. . . . But this is all of yesterday; the leaven works, and every day the movement gains strength.

If there was any real recognition in the nineteenth century of the labourings which preceded the birth of a work of art, it took the form only of a feeling that matters artistic were quite incomprehensible and arrived at their maturity in some haphazard way. As to furniture, there was a total lack of recognition that artistic work is

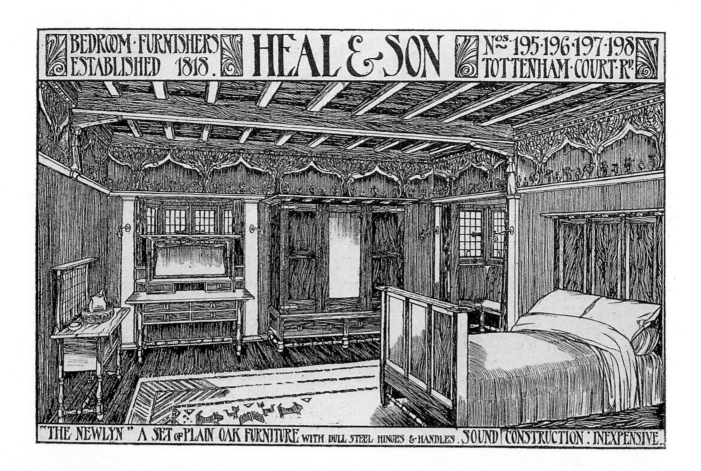

BEDROOM·FURNISHERS· ESTABLISHED 1818· HEAL & SON N°S·195·196·197·198 TOTTENHAM·COURT·R°

"THE·NEWLYN" A SET OF PLAIN OAK FURNITURE WITH DULL STEEL HINGES & HANDLES. SOUND CONSTRUCTION: INEXPENSIVE.

only possible (geniuses excepted) when it reflects the desires and ideals of a period when Beauty is recognised . . . It is only by recognising that artistic work is an outcome of the spirit of the times that we can reach safe ground. If the conditions are favourable, we may hope once again to do good work. If it is to appeal to us as a beautiful thing, it must have some human quality about it. It need not necessarily be made wholly by hand; there may be some concession to cost of production, and there are many ways in which machinery helps in this direction; but to feed wood in at one end of an insatiate monster and expect chefs d'oeuvre at the other is but to court disillusionment . . .

Finally let it be emphasised that cheapness is not the sole end and aim of existence. The definite obligation, if we wish to have furniture that will equal that of the eighteenth century, is to find out more about it, and probe into the conditions of labour and craft that went to produce it. One claims no standard of morality for Art; Benvenuto Cellini was a prodigious scoundrel but a great artist, and he could be the one and yet the other, because he recognised Beauty as an asset. Our civilisation appears to have neglected it, and so we suffer; or do we think that ugliness is more respectable?

FROM 'ARCHITECTURAL FURNITURE', BY

C. H. B. QUENNELL, 1911.

NEW VERNACULAR HOUSING AT ARDELEY IN HERTFORDSHIRE,

DESIGNED BY F. C. EDEN, *c.* 1917.

Architects of the stature of Blow, Prior and Voysey also built cottages in the traditional sense – small homes for working-class people – although they were often part of larger schemes. Prior, for example, created a curious design for a pair of semi-detached cottages at Kelling that have their ground-floor windows and doors set back within huge stone arches. Such idiosyncratic buildings were, of course, the exception. For one thing, they hardly produced an economically viable return. Like Morris before them, architects of the Domestic Revival found that good honest craftsmanship did not come cheap.

As writers waxed lyrical over the romance of an ancient timber-framed house in the country, and advanced architects stipulated that their huge 'cottages' should be finished in sanded oak and matt metalwork, the housing needs of the traditional cottage-dweller continued to exercise the mind and conscience of the nation.

Things were undoubtedly better than they had been in the mid-nineteenth century, although the underlying causes of these improvements themselves gave rise to concern, as F. G. Heath remarked in *British Rural Life and Labour* (1911):

> *One of these reasons [for a decrease in the overcrowding of cottages over the past forty years] is the appreciable increase in more sanitary dwellings; the*

*other is the less satisfactory decline in the rural population brought about by
the untempting conditions of an agricultural labourer's life – for, in spite of
the increase in wages that has taken place during the same period, the fact
remains that the cultivation of the soil in this country does not furnish, now,
attractions sufficient to prevent the steady stream of migration to the towns,
and emigration to our colonies and elsewhere.*

Romantic though it might have appeared to the bourgeois couple in their suburb, life in
the country cottage held few charms for the rural labourer. 'Everywhere,' wrote F. E.
Green in 1913, 'we are face to face with racial degeneracy and depletion of our countryside.' 'Racial denegeracy' was a common cry at the time, when it was thought that within a couple of generations urban living conditions produced an inferior type of worker.
The idea was summed up by Rider Haggard in 1899:

*The city breeds one stamp of human being and the country breeds another . . .
Take the people away from their natural breed and growing grounds, thereby sapping their health and strength in cities such as nature never intended
to be the permanent homes of men, and the decay of this country becomes only
a matter of time.*

Short of forcible repatriation, the best answer seemed to be to persuade the rural worker
to stay on the land. A Select Committee reporting in 1906 suggested that improved housing was a way forward, but not the only way. If the agricultural labourer had the chance
or, just as importantly, felt that he had the chance, of having some land of his own, then
'the exodus from the country might be materially checked'.

SUBSISTENCE FARMING –
NO LONGER A HARSH
WAY OF LIFE, BUT A
PICTURESQUE DREAM.

Various legislation was brought into play, some of it
more effective than others. Smallholdings and Allotments
Acts of 1892 and 1908 attempted to establish a framework
whereby cottagers could become farmers, albeit on a small
scale. The 1913 Small Holdings Committee also set out rec-
ommendations for the minimum size, or sizes, of new cottages – two separate schedules were provided, one for the
smallholder's cottage and another for the rural labourer's. All
ceilings should be at least eight feet high (a standard that was
enshrined in most local housing bye-laws), and the living-
kitchen should be no less than 180 square feet in area, or, in
the case of the labourer's home, 165 square feet. There should
be a scullery and larder, and three bedrooms, the largest
either 150 or 144 square feet and the other two 100 square
feet and sixty-five square feet in both schedules.

Although it helped to introduce the idea of minimum

standards in worker-housing, the smallholdings scheme did little to improve the lot of the ordinary labourer. County Councils, which were given the power to compulsorily purchase land for smallholdings, were often reluctant to do so, dominated as they were by the big farmers. There were some 30,000 smallholders by the 1920s, but many of the holdings were not occupied by cottagers, who had neither the time to cultivate extra land nor the money needed to stock it. Instead, farmers often took advantage of the scheme to provide themselves with extra land, as did country tradesmen who were looking for somewhere to pasture their draught animals.

The Town Planning Act of 1909 allowed for cottage-dwellers to petition for an enquiry if their home was below standard. But here, too, the legislation was hardly an unqualified success. By 1912, 153 new cottages had been built as a result of this legislation. But an enquiry could also lead to a house being judged unfit for habitation, and during the same three-year period 1,689 homes had been served with closure orders. As one commentator noted at the time, the labourer 'may reasonably enough prefer to sleep under a leaky roof rather than on the roadside under an open sky'.

The search continued, however, both for more cottages and for better standards. There was a scheme to halt rural depopulation in Ireland, by building cottages with half an acre or an acre and letting them out at between 8d. and 2s.6d. a week. The shortfall in rents was made up partly by the ratepayers and partly through government subsidy. Its success was such that in 1912 Beville Stanier introduced a Rural Housing Bill into Parliament, with the aim of operating the scheme on the British mainland. Housing Commissioners would establish the demand for cottages in different areas of the country, and would be given the power to compel Rural District Councils to build them. The money would come in the form of Treasury loans, repayable by the builder over a period of sixty-eight years, and rents would be fixed at two shillings a week. Although nothing much came of Stanier's Bill at the time, it did point the way to the only practical solution to the Cottage Problem – new building that was subsidised by local and/or national government through rates and taxes.

As the First World War drew to a close, Lloyd George's government turned its attention to building homes fit for heroes, not least because ignoring the state of worker-housing might lead to Bolshevism, as George V made clear in 1919. 'If unrest is to be converted into contentment,' he had argued, 'the provision of good houses may provide one of the most potent agents in that conversion.'

In the midst of all the dry-as-dust legislation, a 1918 report by a Local Government Board Committee chaired by Sir Tudor Walters is particularly revealing about attitudes towards both urban and rural workers' houses. The Committee found that the desire for a parlour was 'remarkably widespread', so much so that some of the witnesses it heard said they would be willing to put up with a smaller living-kitchen and scullery if only they could have one. No doubt this was partly due to higher aspirations for a bourgeois lifestyle, as Lawrence Weaver noted at the time:

The old argument that parlours are a needless expense because cottagers use them only as a museum for useless furniture, wax flowers and wool mats may surely now be given decent burial, but even if it were true . . . [The] desire for wool mats is an embryonic appreciation of a higher standard of living and of the place of art in the home.

But a parlour had practical uses over and above the status that it conferred. Some thought it necessary as a sanctuary where parents could talk with their friends without being interrupted by children; others said that it could be used as a sick-room, or a place where youngsters could do their homework. 'It is generally required for home lessons by the children of school age, or for similar work of study, serious reading, or writing, on the part of any member of the family.' Rational recreation still loomed large in most thinking about working-class leisure during the early twentieth century, although paradoxically the compulsory schooling brought about by a series of Education Acts was a source of discontent among rural rate-payers who felt that they were funding the education of cottagers' children, only for the brightest of those children to leave for the towns.

The desire for a parlour, which continued in spite of Weaver's hopes to be essentially a room that was kept for the best occasions, had repercussions for the rest of the planning of a modern cottage. There was a growing tendency in those cottages that already possessed parlours for the day-to-day life of the household to be carried on in the living-kitchen. As a result cooking was banished to the scullery, although this meant extra expense in keeping alight both a cooking range in the scullery and an open fire in the living-kitchen. (A fire was only lit in the parlour on special occasions.) In the later nineteenth century the bath was usually kept in the scullery, where water and drainage were already laid on and where the copper could provide hot water. But as the scullery became to all intents and purposes a working kitchen, it was more and more inconvenient to have it closed off while members of the family bathed, especially where it provided the only means of access from the living-kitchen to the larder, coal-store and back door. The Walters Committee recommended that bathrooms should be separate from, but next door to, the scullery, so that the copper could continue to provide hot water: 'Upstairs bathrooms were ruled out because of the cost in running supplies of hot

A SLATE-QUARRIER AND HIS FAMILY IN THEIR COTTAGE HOME, 1946.

and cold water to the first floor.' Where it was absolutely necessary to put a bath in the scullery, 'it should be fitted with a hinged table-top as cover, and this may serve as one of the ledges adjacent to the sink'.

All these proposals – in fact, all of the good intentions regarding the provision of decent cottages – foundered on the question of money. The problem was the same as it had been in the nineteenth century. It cost x number of pounds to build a decent cottage. The rural worker could only afford to pay y shillings a week in rent. If x were £250, say, and y were two shillings, a landlord or a speculative builder was looking at an annual return on his or her investment of just over two per cent, out of which he or she would have to find money for repairs. It was not worth it.

Not unnaturally, discussion focussed on the issue of cost. Was it possible to build a cottage for a sufficiently small sum to make it economically viable, while still providing a standard of accommodation that was high enough to meet a labourer's expectations and keep him and his family on the land?

In the years before the First World War, the dream was a cottage that might be built for less than £150 – the most a landowner could afford to spend, assuming that he could expect to receive no more than three shillings a week in rent. It proved rather elusive. In 1906, Percy Houfton's design for a £150 three-bedroomed cottage won first prize in a competition for cheap cottages in the garden city at Letchworth. It consisted of a detached rectangular block in roughcast brick about twenty-five by nineteen feet, with deal woodwork. There was no parlour. One half of the ground floor was filled with a living room (nineteen by twelve feet) and the other half by a scullery-kitchen, an indoor WC and a coal store under the stairs. But the costs were held down artificially,

£150 COTTAGE.

THE LAND CO., 68 Cheapside, E.C.

THE DREAM OF MANY BUILDERS BEFORE WWI WAS THE £150 COTTAGE.

since Houfton did not include a sum for the architect's or builder's profit. Commercially, Houfton was only able to build his low-cost cottage for £250, or £400 a pair – figures that placed them out of the reach of rural labourers and raised them into the 'weekend retreat' category.

The Letchworth competition also yielded an interesting cottage by Lionel Crane. It was timber-framed on a brick base, with a jettied upper storey, and was clad on the outside in weatherboard and internally faced in plaster. But at £175, it failed to meet the price criterion. Another pair built at Letchworth, this time by Philip Baillie Scott, are particularly attractive, with wide, sweeping roofs and a central recessed porch. But at £500 the pair they too were outside the traditional cottager's range, and a pre-war photograph of a self-consciously Arts and Crafts interior with its spindly Morris& Co. furniture, a valance over the fireplace and a pair of quaint little wall sconces suggests that it was occupied by a reader of *The Lady* rather than by an agricultural labourer.

The search for a cheap cottage led, not surprisingly, to various experiments with cheaper materials. St Loe Strachey of the *Spectator*, a tireless advocate of cheap housing for the rural worker, produced a pair of cottages on Merrow Down for £300, using concrete blocks and pantiles. They were by no means as awful to look at as the description suggests, although the accommodation they provided was quite basic. They were small, (around seventeen by nineteen feet) and did not contain a parlour – 'a symbol of a higher standard of living,' said one critic, 'and as such [it] has some moral value.' There was no water supply laid on apart from a rainwater butt, and most of the interior walls were left unplastered. Like Houfton's attempt at the £150 cottage, Strachey's houses could hardly be reproduced elsewhere for the same price, since he, too, underestimated architect's and builder's fees, which would have brought the true cost up to about £330 the pair.

At Garboldisham on the Norfolk-Suffolk border, Percy Morley Horder's own quest for a cheap alternative to brick and stone led to a square two-bedroom bungalow cottage built from clay lump. This material had a rather longer lineage than concrete, in East Anglia at least. For centuries in the area around Thetford and Diss clay had been mixed with straw, trodden, pressed into wooden moulds and left to dry, forming large blocks that were mortared in place and either rendered with lime plaster or covered with tar that was sanded and colour-washed.

The early-twentieth-century desire to produce rural housing that paid lip-service in some way or another to the vernacular, by either using traditional materials or traditional forms, or both, was very much a product of the Arts and Crafts movement. Modern design and modern building practice were seen as simply inappropriate to cottage-building, and although experiments were made before the First World War with

BUDGET DESIGNS FOR COTTAGES WERE NEVER A FEASIBLE OPTION FOR THE RURAL LABOURER.

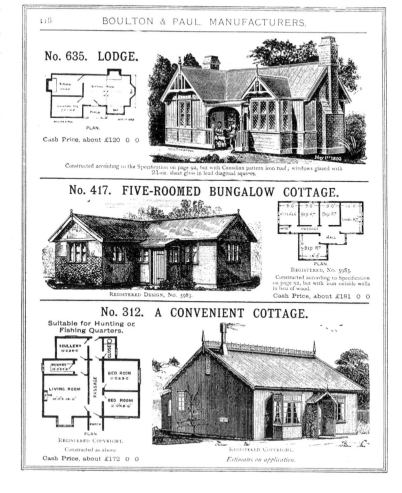

EDWARDIAN LOW-COST (£100) COTTAGE AT MERROW DOWN.

THE COST-CUTTING RESULTS OF UTTER SIMPLICITY IN DESIGN

AND SPARING USE OF ORNAMENTATION.

poured and reinforced concrete, they were generally frowned upon. 'The directions in which cottage-building may possibly develop with some economic advantage,' wrote Lawrence Weaver in 1913, 'such as by the use of concrete in monolithic form, either reinforced or not, do not seem compatible with architectural charm.' And charm was the essence of the English country cottage. Never mind that the internal walls went unplastered or that rain was the only water supply. So long as the cottage *looked* like a cottage should look from the outside, and provided just enough in the way of accommodation and comfort to prevent the cottager from leaving to look for work in the city, everyone was happy. Everyone but the cottager, that is. The Picturesque was a long time dying.

The association between tradition and the cottage seemed to militate against the emergence of any real new aesthetic during the first forty years of the century. There is a remarkable passage in the 1926 edition of Weaver's seminal work on the state of English

cottage building, *Cottages – Their Planning, Design and Materials*, in which it seems, just for a moment, that all the cultural baggage that the cottage had been carrying for the past 150 years was finally about to be discarded:

CLEAN, SIMPLE COTTAGE FURNISHING, BY ARTS AND CRAFTS DESIGNER GORDON RUSSEL.

> *I know there are still people who think that beauty lurks in barge boards and little oriel windows and the quirks and tricks of the pre-war speculative builder which can be catalogued as 'quaint', but their number is growing less. The attempt at prettiness has too long been the curse of architecture, the attempt to capture the elusive beauty of craftmanship of past centuries in our day, when the men and the social organism of which they were a part have passed into the limbo of history.*

However, lest anyone make the mistake of thinking that the conservative Weaver was rubbing shoulders with Gropius and Le Corbusier, he executes an abrupt about-turn with his very next breath:

> *The public taste has happily set steadily in a return to eighteenth-century traditions, and we have the right to be Georgian in our houses as in our loy-*

alties. For the eighteenth century was the Age of Reason, and to that our architecture is returning.

The deep-rooted architectural contextualism that for good or bad dictated architectural fashion in the countryside could not of course, exclude the new. But it could, and did, heap scorn on those cottages that broke with the rural idyll. Writing admiringly of a pair of Tudoresque cottages designed for a site at Painswick in Gloucestershire by Sydney Barnsley around the time of the First World War, St Clair Baddeley compared them with the red and yellow brick, blue-slated, vermillion-ridged horrors that were appearing elsewhere in the neighbourhood. 'The latest specimen in this insulting style has been stuck down only seven years ago beside the high road between Painswick and Stroud,' he wrote, 'face to face with a picturesque old inn, happily to the great distaste of the entire neighbourhood.' In contrast, Barnsley's cottages, high gabled and built in a creamy local stone to an unusual L-shaped plan, had a 'traditional beauty of line, colour and mouldings . . . The delicate curve in the stone door-heads and dripstones sufficiently recalls their Tudor derivation.' They might have been new, but they did not look it.

This yearning for a sense of place was at the heart of a letter to *Country Life* written just before the outbreak of war by Lord Curzon, bemoaning the demolition of old cottages:

> *It would be a national tragedy if these old buildings were to be replaced by a new standardised cottage, dumped down either singly or – still worse – in rows like a lot of band-boxes, or canisters, or dog-kennels. The best way to prevent such a catastrophe seems to me to lie in the preparation of plans, sketches and models of cottages of different materials and styles, suitable to differences of locality, climate and surroundings.*

The result was another *Country Life* competition. Architects were to design a pair of cottages costing no more than £250 the pair, for particular localities, producing homes that conformed to the schedule for the minimum size of a rural labourer's cottage set down by the 1913 Small Holdings Committee. Eighteen landowners agreed to build the prize-winning design for their local type.

Sadly, the war put an effective halt to the idea of implementing the designs, and most went unbuilt. But some did see the light of day. The first prize went to Alex Harvey and Graham Wicks for a plain but pleasing scheme. It was basically a two-up, two-down, except that whereas the living-kitchen filled the front on the ground floor, the space behind it was divided into a small scullery and a third bedroom. There was a single door to the side and a shared single-storey block behind, containing pairs of fuel stores and earth closets. The most distinctive feature was the pantiled Mansard roof that dropped down to just above the level of the ground-floor windows, with dormers to light the two upstairs bedrooms and the little landing.

Harvey's and Wicks' cottages were built in 1916 just outside Grantham by

THE FACT THAT SO MANY COTTAGES WERE BEING DEMOLISHED, OR SIMPLY
LEFT TO FALL DOWN MADE THEM SEEM ALL THE MORE PRECIOUS. THE
EARTH CLOSET (BELOW RIGHT) WOULD SOON BE REPLACED BY THE WC.

Christopher Turnor, the moving force behind the Small Holdings Committee. Turnor ended up paying £350 16s.7d. for the two rather than the estimated £250, but this, he admitted, was partly his own fault, since he decided against the architects' choice of reinforced concrete for walls and floor:

> *£30 17s.11d. was absorbed by the use of very attractive buff bricks and hand-made tiles, which add much to the architectural charm of the cottages, but nothing to their efficiency as homes. One has to suffer in pocket sometimes for the determination to preserve local colour. I have not got my cottages for £125 each, but they are well planned and built, very popular with their tenants, and an ornament rather than an eyesore.*

Here and there other architects also indulged in external ornament. Examples include the diapered brickwork of the chimney stack and the panels of pargetting that Kieffer and Fleming applied to cottages built at Elmdon in Essex for the local RDC; and the rather large roundel containing its owner's initials and the date, 1914, that H. W. Hobbiss built at Newport in the same county. The desire to produce cheap cottages that still preserved 'local colour' did not really lead to the renaissance of the Age of Reason that Lawrence Weaver had looked forward to. Higher

OLD COTTAGE, LINGFIELD, SURREY – THE CULT OF THE ANTIQUE 'HAS ALL BUT PETERED OUT IN A SURREY LANE AND A TOTTENHAM COURT ROAD JUNKSHOP'.

up the social scale, people in the 1910s and 1920s continued to flirt with dreams of Olde Englande. Photographs taken in the late 1920s of a cottage called The Needles, just outside Horsham, show a rambling timber-framed house that is almost entirely a modern construct. A ruined farmhouse had its plaster stripped away to expose the timbers and the windows filled with new lattice panes, and all the new work was carried out using old materials. Inside the rooms were filled with antiques, reminding one of Harry Batsford's remark in 1938 that the cult of the antique 'has all but petered out in a Surrey Lane and a Tottenham Court Road junkshop'. A four-poster bed was installed, a spinning wheel was set beside the huge (and brand-new) open fire; a grandfather clock stood in the corner of what used to be a coal cellar. An electricity generator was installed in the garden, along with a lych-gate and a dovecote. Florentine light-fittings were found suitable because they were 'reproductions of thirteenth-century ironwork, of beautiful design coeval with that of the cottage, which is supposed to date from twelve hundred and something', as P. A. Barron wrote in *The House Desirable* (1929). He also claims that 'modern electric candles, with well-chosen shades, do not look out of place in the old candlesticks and sconces.' The Needles is beautiful, but both its restoration and its interior furnishings say much more about the twentieth century's obsession with the past than about historic cottages, as do most modern 'cottages' illustrated in Barron's fascinating book. They range from the spectacularly irregular 'old-world house' built by Blunden Shadbolt at Betchworth, 'an excellent example of a house newly built in such manner that it has the appearance of great age', to the group of cottages designed and built by Tiles & Potteries Ltd at West Chiltington near Pulborough, with wavy thatch, timber-framed upper storeys and integral garages. There is a certain irony in the fact that the detached motor-houses described by Barron (in a chapter called 'The Garage Desirable'), with their weatherboarded or oak-timbered walls and their roofs of Horsham stone or Norfolk thatch, are considerably better appointed, but about the same size, as labourers' cottages of the previous century.

Most of the country cottages built between the wars, however, had none of these refinements. It became clear that for all the competitions and campaigns, the provision of low-cost rural housing could not be left to well-meaning private individuals, and county councils became the major builders, much to the horror of most commentators. 'Mean little "council houses" . . . seem nowadays to perch with such malevolent intention to spoil the patch of country in which they stand', said Batsford. 'County Council cottages,' declared Barron, 'are the most hideous of all buildings erected within the memory of man.' It seemed to many that councils took the view that the provision of warm, dry accommodation at a low cost, with decent sanitation and a clean water supply, could only be achieved at the expense of individuality and picturesque design. What was even more galling was that country families were usually delighted to desert their quaint tumbledown cottages to live in the new authority housing, knowing from bitter experience the truth of Chesterton's remark that 'rose-covered cottages should not colour our conception too much. The roses are all outside such places; the thorns are within.'

Rural communities in England were undergoing drastic change in the post-war period that went far beyond the erection of utilitarian council cottages. The break-up of many of the great estates as a result of death duties and taxation led to a transfer of social and economic power to a new class of owner-farmers, former tenants who bought up the farms that the aristocracy were forced to sell. The abolition in 1921 of wartime guaran-

PREWAR COTTAGES AT FREEFOLK, HAMPSHIRE, ATTEST TO THE
CONTINUING APPEAL OF THE PICTURESQUE.

IN VILLAGE AFTER VILLAGE, COTTAGES WERE NO LONGER OCCUPIED BY
PEOPLE WHO WORKED ON THE LAND, BUT BY NEWCOMERS FROM THE CITY.

teed prices in the face of a resumption of wheat imports from abroad meant a corresponding fall in agricultural wages, which even at their height had only been around fifty per cent of the national wage. More importantly, the recessions of the 1920s caused farmers both to lay off workers and to mechanize wherever possible. Tractors replaced men and horses, and reaper-binders did away with the need for hand harvesting. In the mid-nineteenth century, one in five of the whole population was employed in agriculture, but by 1924 this figure had dropped by almost two-thirds, to one in fourteen.

Inevitably, the flight from the land that Edwardian social theorists had feared so much continued. S. L. Bensusan, who toured the countryside in 1927 gathering material for his book, *Latter Day Rural England*, saw village after village where cottages were occupied no longer by people who worked on the land, but by incomers:

> *Thirty years ago all these cottages belonged to the agricultural labourers, who paid from fifteen pence to two shillings a week rent; today, where they are rented, they fetch from £20 to £30 a year . . . Because they have been divorced from their proper ownership the young men and women of the village must emigrate or seek the slums.*

For those who stayed behind, traditional cultural pursuits were overwhelmed by the march of progress, although often to the villagers' advantage. Regular bus services gave them access to shops and cinemas in the towns, and widened their social circle. The wireless brought an homogenized culture that tended to even out local and regional differences. It was left to middle-class outsiders to record the vanishing cottages, the oral traditions and folk-songs, to eulogize a disappearing world; and as the mid-twentieth century has proved, the new rural England – and the country cottage that symbolized it – would from that moment on belong to them.

REAL LIFE IN THE COTTAGE AFTER THE SECOND WORLD WAR. A COUPLE
HAVE TAKEN OVER THIS PEMBROKESHIRE FARM (1946). THE FIREPLACE
BUILT INSIDE THE OLD CHIMNEY WAS THEIR ADDITION.

A Place in the Country

*In the modern old-fashioned cottage one has the outward semblance of a
primitive simplicity, while inside are the latest modern appliances. The roof
is thatched, but there is a telephone wire running from it. The kitchen is
used for a living-room, and we are studiously medieval in the matter of set-
tles and trestle-tables, but we switch on the electric light when required,
and the bath-room is supplied with hot and cold water.*

STEWART DICK, *THE COTTAGE HOMES OF ENGLAND*, 1909

Over the last fifty years or so, the strain of anti-urbanism that runs backwards
through the work of the architects of the Domestic Revival, through the writings of Morris and Ruskin to the Romantic poets and beyond, has grown to
such an extent that life in the country cottage, with all that that phrase represents, has
acquired an almost mythical status. Firms specializing exclusively in renting out country
cottages offer the chance to spend a fortnight, a week or just an offpeak weekend break,
actually living in a dream-world where, according to their brochures, 'supper is laid upon
the scrubbed pine table, with blue patterned crockery from the tall eighteenth-century
dresser. The white walls and exposed beams catch the golden glow of late slanting sunlight.' And the old-world charm is tempered by the provision of en-suite bathrooms,
colour televisions, microwaves, dishwashers and tumble-dryers.

*THE COTTAGE HOME, BY
WILLIAM H. SNAPE
ILLUSTRATES LATE-
VICTORIAN SENTIMENT.*

We have come a long way from the labourer's cottage of the nineteenth century, with
its water supply in a ditch outside the door and its privy no more than a hole in the back
yard. And thank God we have. Our yearning for the simple rural life has more in common with the builders of Georgian *cottages
ornées*, taking us back to Malton, Pocock
and the need to provide 'the necessary
conveniences for persons of refined manners and habits'. But a yearning it unques-
tionably is, for the past, for the countryside, for life in a small community with a
pub, a post office and a church, even if we
only set foot inside its doors at Christmas.
Part of the appeal can be attributed to a
vastly increased urban population continuing to idealize country life. By the 1980s
over ninety per cent of the population of
England and Wales were living in urban
areas. But more practical considerations are
just as important, in particular the increased
access that town-dwellers have to the countryside. At the beginning of this century,

20189 Orion S_143

those who were able to take a holiday every summer were regarded as extremely fortunate. By the 1930s those who could not take a least a week were regarded as extremely unfortunate. And in the 1990s four weeks' annual leave is the norm, while well over eighty per cent work a five-day week. Car ownership, which allows the town-dweller the freedom to explore the countryside, rose from around 250,000 in 1919 to nearly 1.5 million in 1929; by the late 1980s there were more than 18 million cars and 31 million licences held.

These two factors enabled more and more people to get away from the towns. In the words of the *Autocar Road Book* of 1910, they could discover 'not only all the most outstanding places with which it behoves those who love their country to be acquainted, but also a very large proportion of those less-known hamlets and rural districts which, not yet *exploités*, should give the traveller who comes, delighted, to their unspoiled beauties, something of the thrilful experience of an explorer'. And for those who did not have access to a car there was, before Beeching's drastic cuts in the rail network of the 1960s and the reduction in bus routes in the 1980s, a comprehensive public transportation system. At 3d. each, the three collections of *Country Walks*, which were first published by London Transport in 1936 and in print for the next thirty years provided everything the Londoner needed to know in order to undertake some 770 miles of rambles in the countryside around the capital. There was fare information, underground stations, Green Line coach routes, advice on correct behaviour ('Make as little noise as possible when you pass through a village in the evening', 'Avoid, if possible, making enquiries at a farmhouse or mill on a Sunday afternoon'), a countryside glossary that explained the meaning of such terms as 'forest' and 'common' and even some suitably uplifting lines from William Morris:

> *From township to township, o'er down and by tillage*
> *Far, far have we wandered and long was the day,*
> *But now cometh eve at the end of the village*
> *Where over the grey wall the church riseth grey.*

The Home Counties England that these walks explored was filled with quaint oddities and rural charm: kissing-gates where 'the bold swain was wont to demand toll of the bashful damsel on the other side of the gate', village stocks, curious inn-signs, ancient manor houses – and, of course, cottages:

> *MATCHING GREEN, a big, rough green, with a duckpond. Encircling the green*
> *is a rare assortment of rustic cottages – some weather-boarded, some brick,*
> *some plastered, some tiled, some thatched, some with dormers, some without*
> *– no two alike! On the east a signboard marks the Chequers (teas).*

Alongside such innocent yet wholly delightful joy in the sight of a group of cottages – a response unencumbered by knowledge – went a more serious side, a feeling that the rural landscape was being vandalized. Old cottages were being demolished or left to decay. The old, the unspoilt, the real England would soon be lost forever.

'Practically all the country we walk over is somebody's private property,' said one travel-writer on the eve of the Second World War. 'But it also happens to be every Englishman's heritage. It is our privilege still to enjoy most of the land that the builder has not savaged.' The war itself did a great deal to confirm this notion that rural England was the real England, that life in the country cottage was Englishness at its best. The villages portrayed in films like *Mrs Miniver, Went the Day Well?* and *A Canterbury Tale* reminded people of what they were fighting for every bit as effectively as stirring flag-wavers such as Olivier's *Henry V*, even if those villages were ultimately as far removed from the reality of ordinary people's lives as the battle of Agincourt. So powerful, indeed, were the more general images of a picturesque rural England that people began to go to extraordinary lengths to force the reality to fit the myth. One common example of this is brilliantly caricatured by Osbert Lancaster in his 1949 'history' of the imaginary town of Drayneflete:

OLD WARDEN, BEDFORDSHIRE, WAS 'IMPROVED' BY LORD ONGLEY IN THE MID-19TH CENTURY.

Still stranger, perhaps, than their disregard of the claims of antiquity was the seventeenth-century public's unawareness of the true beauty of their own buildings; thus many of the fine old half-timbered houses erected during this period were covered by a flat wash of common plaster. Fortunately, more enlightened ideas prevail today and the Council has been at great pains to strip off this outer covering on such houses of that date as have now survived, thus revealing for the first time the full beauty of the glorious old oak beams.

The inhabitants of Drayneflete, like their neighbours in a thousand villages and small towns in rural England, were imitating art with a vengeance, and in the process replacing aesthetically pleasing, historically correct and practical weatherproofing with the Hollywood vernacular of *Mrs Miniver*. That practice continues today.

It should be emphasized that not everyone agreed the cottage *should* be preserved. For a more progressive and hardheaded element in mid-twentieth-century society, a regret that the decline of the cottage tradition 'represents the decline of elements which we can ill afford to obliterate from our national life' was a luxury that we really could not afford. A much more important priority was the provision of decent housing for rural workers, and the consensus was that existing cottages simply could not fit the bill. Frank Sykes, writing about the state of farming in 1944, put this side of the argument succinctly. The old cottages in his own village had already been altered to make them more convenient: two or three had been knocked into one, dormer windows had been put in, electricity and water had been laid on. But they still did not meet present housing needs:

A house is like an engine designed to do a certain job; once the engine is built, it is no good adding a few cylinders afterwards: in order to get extra power, a new engine must be designed if it is to function properly. An architect can remodel an old cottage, but he can never make it as habitable as a new one.

Others agreed with Sykes. The agricultural economist C. S. Orwin ended his *Problems of the Countryside* (1945) with a utopian vision of village life as seen by a new Rip Van Winkle who has fallen asleep in 1940 and woken a generation hence. The isolated cottages in the fields, 'remote from neighbours, public services and the amenities of village life' have all disappeared. So, too, have the fields themselves. Their hedgerows and ditches have all been swept away to create much larger fields. The village itself is filled with new houses, larger than the old and each with a good garden, and farmworkers live in them and travel to work on motorbikes. There is a health clinic, a library, a canteen and restaurant and adult education classrooms. The little village school has been replaced by a new, larger building, and the wheelwright's shop has given way to a branch of the local Cooperative Society. 'Rip Van Winkle had an impression of a virile, well-knit society . . . And he found it good.'

The tumbledown labourer's cottage had no part to play in this utilitarian brave new world. Frank Sykes had an answer. 'The farm labourer wants a new house: sell his old one to a townsman who would not live in anything built since Cromwell's day'.

Things may not have quite worked out according to plan. There are still plenty of farmworkers and their families living in cramped, substandard accommodation, and well into the 1960s it was possible to find isolated cottages with no mains water or electricity,

SIR THOMAS ACKLAND REBUILT SELWORTHY IN SOMERSET IN 1828 AS A PICTURESQUE VILLAGE
TO PROVIDE HOUSING FOR THE PENSIONERS ON HIS ESTATE.

where cooking was done with Calorgas and a twelve-volt car battery powered a TV set. But car ownership and a deepening contempt for (and fear of) urban life have led many middle-class families to move into an old cottage of their own while continuing to work in the towns and cities.

And an *old* cottage it almost always is, even when the 'cottage' is a substantial house far removed from the labourers' homes of the past. The cottage has become synonymous with age – so much so that the idea of building a brand-new cottage in the 1990s seems rather curious. Those that appeared in the various experimental villages of the last decade or so are products of the reaction to modernism, pastiches of historic styles trying rather desperately to maintain or recreate architectural traditions that are well past their sell-by date.

'THE VILLAGE ITSELF IS FILLED WITH NEW HOUSES, LARGER THAN THE OLD AND EACH WITH A GOOD GARDEN.'

❧ ❧ ❧

Life in the country cottage goes on, of course. But it tends to involve a difficult and often heartbreaking process of compromise and adjustment. Take, for example, as a rather dangerously anecdotal piece of evidence, the village in Somerset where I live. It consists of about seventy houses, most of which would be described both today and when they were built as 'cottages'. Made of stone with slate roofs, they span some three hundred years, from the Stuart farmhouse – one of the few larger houses in the village – that was converted into two dwellings at some point (and has recently been converted back again), to the terraces of two-up, two-down cottages that dominate the area and were built to house a growing population of coal-miners in the late nineteenth and early twentieth centuries. There has been some infilling – an Edwardian smallholding was built over with a pair of semi-detached houses in the 1970s, for example – and the sky is now criss-crossed with overhead power lines. But by and large the village seems to have remained substantially as it was in the years before the First World War.

Some of the old families still occupy the homes that their grandparents and great-grandparents lived in. Although the pits closed half a century ago, traditions survive, and legends of mining disasters and strikes and the impact they had on the community linger on. One night early this century a band of strikers converged on the overseer's house, led by the local Methodist minister. A stone thrown through his window killed the overseer's parrot, and then he retaliated by shooting four strikers with his shotgun. The minister got six months in gaol. I still remember in the early 1980s one of my neighbours, whose father had been a miner, telling me the names of the four men in the village who blacklegged during the 1926 strike. 'For years, no one spoke to them or their families,' he said. 'It's not so bad now, but the families still don't get invited into our homes.'

Although there is an apparent continuity in the village, it is only apparent. The vast majority of villagers are now owner-occupiers. Most, like myself, have moved in only in the last decade. Hardly anybody works within walking distance of their home. Twenty years ago the village could boast a pub, a butcher's shop, a general store and two Methodist chapels. Today only one of the chapels survives; the other buildings have all been convert-ed into houses. The lane is full of parked cars – most families have two – and those cot-tages that have front gardens have tended to lose their low stone garden walls to make room for some off-the-road hard standing. There are burglar alarms under the eaves, and satel-lite dishes are starting to join the television aerials that range along the rooftops.

But the changes to the cottages have gone much further than this. My own 'cottage' is in fact two houses knocked together. Many of the others have been extended at the rear to provide bathrooms and decent-sized kitchens. The long strips of garden that slope down to the valley have all lost their stone-built pigsties, privies and coal stores. There are still some vegetable plots, but most have been wholly or partly grassed. Inside, plaster has been stripped off to expose stonework that was never meant to be seen, and fireplaces have been torn out to reveal stone lintels that had been covered since they were hoisted into place.

'FORGOTTEN HUMBLE HORDES' – PEASANTS MERRYMAKING IN A BARN.

Architectural vandalism? A lack of respect for the past? Perhaps. But ours is a living village, not a theme park. Like most vil-lages, it never was pretty or picturesque. There is no village green, no quaint old church, no duck pond. And all that the cottagers have done is what cottagers have always done – move with the times, as changing tastes dictate and their means allow. It may be sad that parked cars and power lines dominate the landscape, or ironic that the exposed stonework and stripped pine interiors owe more to myth and maga-zines than to architectural correctness. But at least the English cottage is alive and well here. And for the cottage to have a future, it *must* adapt. Otherwise it will be relegated to a museum of rural life, an object of curiosity rather than what it should be – a home.

Addy, S. O., *The Evolution of the English House*, Allen & Unwin (1933).

Aikin, Edmund, *Designs for Villas and other Rural Buildings*, London (1808).

Alison, Archibald, *Essays on the Nature and Principles of Taste*, London (1790).

Allen, B. Sprague, *Tides in English Taste*, Pageant Books (1958).

Andrews, C. Bruyn (ed.), *The Torrington Diaries*, Methuen (1970).

Arch, Joseph, *Joseph Arch: The Story of his Life, Told by Himself*, Hutchinson (1898).

Armstrong, W. A., 'The Workfolk', in G. E. Mingay (ed.), *The Victorian Countryside*, Routledge & Kegan Paul (1981).

Ashby, M. K., *The Changing English Village*, Roundwood (1974).

Ashton, T. S., *An Economic History of England: The Eighteenth Century*, Methuen (1955).

Aslet, Clive, *The Last Country Houses*, Yale (1982).

Atkinson, William, *Views of Picturesque Cottages with Plans*, London (1805).

Barley, M. W., *The English Farmhouse and Cottage*, Routledge & Kegan Paul (1961).

Barnett, D. C., 'Allotments and the Problem of Rural Poverty, 1780-1840', in E. L. Jones and G. E. Mingay (eds.), *Land, Labour and Population in the Industrial Revolution*, Arnold (1967).

Barron, P. A., *The House Desirable: a Handbook for those who Wish to Acquire Homes that Charm*, Methuen (1929).

Batsford, Harry and Christopher Fry, *The English Cottage*, Batsford (1938).

Bean, J. M. W., 'Plague, Population and Economic Decline in England in the Later MiddleAages', *Economic History Review*, 2nd series, 15 (1962-3).

Bedford, Duke of, *A Great Agricultural Estate*, John Murray (1897).

Bennett, E. N., *Problems of Village Life*, Williams & Norgate (1914).

Bensusan, S. L., *Latter Day Rural England*, Edinburgh (1927).

Beresford, M. W. and J. G. Hurst (eds.), *Deserted Medieval Villages*, London (1971).

Beresford, M. W., *The Lost Villages of England*, London (1965).

Bland, A. E, P. A. Browne. and R.H. Tawney (eds.), *English Economic History*, G. Bell & Sons (1914).

Bowler, Ian R., 'The Agricultural Pattern', in Gardiner, Vince and R. J. Johnston, *The Changing Geography of the United Kingdom*, 2nd edn., Routledge (1991).

Brown, R. J., *The English Country Cottage*, Robert Hale (1979).

Brunskill, R. W., *Illustrated Handbook of Vernacular Architecture*, Faber & Faber (1970).

Bülow, Gottfried von (tr.), 'Journey through England and Scotland made by Pupold von Wedel in the years 1584 and 1585,' *Transactions of the Royal Historical Society*, new series 9 (1895).

Bülow, Gottfried von (tr.), 'Diary of the Journey of Philip Julius, Duke of Stettin-Pomerania, through England in the year 1602', *Transactions of the Royal Historical Society*, new series 6 (1892).

Burke, Edmund, *A Philosophical Enquiry into the Origins of our Ideas of the Sublime and the Beautiful*, 2nd edn., London (1787).

Burnett, John, 'Country Diet', in G. E. Mingay (ed.), *The Victorian Countryside*, Routledge & Kegan Paul (1981).

Byrne, M. St Clare, *Elizabethan Life in Town and Country*, 6th edn., Methuen (1950).

Caird, James, *English Agriculture in 1850-51*, Longman (1852).

Cantor, L. M (ed.), *The English Medieval Landscape*, London (1982).

Carew, Richard, *Survey of Cornwall* (1602).

Clark, G. Kitson, *The Making of Victorian England*, Methuen (1962).

Claxton, William J., *Rambles in Rural England*, George G. Harrap (1915).

Clayton-Payne, Andrew and Brent Elliott, *Victorian Flower Gardens*, Weidenfeld and Nicolson (1988).

Clayton-Payne, Andrew, *Victorian Cottages*, Weidenfeld and Nicolson (1993).

Clifton-Taylor, Alec, *The Pattern of English Building*, 4th edn., Faber and Faber (1987).

Cobbett, William, *Rural Rides*, Penguin (1985).

Colman, Sylvia, 'Houses into cottages', *Vernacular Architecture*, 12 (1981).

Colvin, Howard, *A Biographical Dictionary of British Architects 1600-1840*, John Murray (1978).

Committee of Council on Health, Sixth Report of Medical Officer to, (1864).

Cook, Olive, and Edwin Smith, *English Cottages and Farmhouses*, Thames & Hudson (1954).

Cornish, J. G., *Reminiscences of Country Life*, Country Life (1939).

Cornish, Vaughan, *The Scenery of England*, Council for the Preservation of Rural England (1932).

Corran, H., *A History of Brewing*, David & Charles (1975).

Crosland, T. W. H., *The Country Life*, Greening & Co (1906).

Crossley, F. W., *Timber Building in England from Early Times to the end of the Seventeeth Century*, Batsford (1951).

Darley, Gillian, *Villages of Vision*, Architectural Press (1975).

Davey, Norman, *A History of Building Materials,* Phoenix House (1961).

Davie, W. G. & Green, W. Curtis, *Old Cottages and Farmhouses in Surrey*, Batsford (1908).

Davie, W. G. and E. G. Dawber, *Old*

Cottages and Farmhouses in the Cotswold District, Batsford (1906).

Davie, W. G. and E. G. Dawber, *Old Cottages and Farmhouses in Kent and Surrey*, Batsford (1906).

Davies, M. F., *Life in an English Village*, T. Fisher Unwin (1909).

Defoe, Daniel, *A Tour Through the Whole Island of Great Britain*, Everyman (1962).

Dent, J. D., 'The Present Condition of the English Agricultural Labourer', *Journal of the Royal Agricultural Society*, 2nd series, VII (1871).

Dick, Oliver Lawson (ed.), *Aubrey's Brief Lives*, Mandarin (1992).

Dick, Stewart, *The Cottage Homes of England*, Edward Arnold (1909).

Digby, A., 'The Rural Poor Law', in D. Fraser (ed.), *The New Poor Law in the Nineteenth Century*, Macmillan (1976).

Ditchfield, P. H., and Fred Roe, *Vanishing England*, 2nd edn., Methuen (1911).

Ditchfield, P. H., *The Cottages and the Village Life of Rural England*, J. M. Dent (1912).

Eden, Sir Frederick, *The State of the Poor* (1746).

Elton, G. R., *England Under the Tudors*, 2nd edn., Methuen (1985).

Ernle, Lord (Rowland Prothero), *English Farming Past and Present*, Longman Green (1912).

Estienne, Charles, *Maison Rustique* or *The Country Farm*, tr. Richard Surfleet and rev. Gervase Markham (1616).

'Eunice', 'Home Decoration: A Simple Cottage', *The Lady*, 29 August 1895.

Evans, Tony and Candida Lycett Green, *English Cottages*, Weidenfeld and Nicolson (1982).

Eversley, Lord (G. S. Lefevre), 'The Decline in the Number of Agricultural Labourers in Great Britain', *Journal of the Royal Statistical Society*, LXX (1907).

Faulkner, P. A., 'Domestic Planning from the Twelfth to the Fourteenth Centuries', *Archaeological Journal*, CXV (1958).

Fawcett, Henry, *The Economic Position of the English Labourer*, Macmillan (1865).

Fiennes, Celia, *The Journeys of Celia Fiennes*, Macdonald (1983).

Fitzherbert, J., *The Book of Husbandry of Master Fitzherbert* (1534).

Furnivall, F. J. (ed.), *Elizabethan England* (William Harrison's Description of England), Walter Scott (1877).

Gandy, Joseph, *Designs for Cottages, Cottage Farms and other Rural Buildings*, London (1805).

Gandy, Joseph, *The Rural Architect*, London (1805).

Gauldie, Enid, 'Country Homes', in G. E. Mingay (ed.), *The Victorian Countryside*, Routledge & Kegan Paul (1981).

Gebhard, David, *Charles F. A. Voysey, Architect*, Los Angeles (1975).

Gilpin, William, *Observations on the Western Parts of England*, London (1798).

Gilpin, William, *Three Essays: on Picturesque Beauty; on Picturesque Travel; and on Sketching Landscape*, 3rd edn., London (1808).

Girouard, Mark, The *Victorian Country House*, Yale (1979).

Gloag, John, *A Social History of Furniture Design*, Cassell (1966).

Gloag, John, *Mr Loudon's England*, Oriel (1970).

Goodwin, Francis, *Domestic Architecture*, London (1833).

Graham, P. Anderson, *The Rural Exodus: The Problem of the Village and the Town*, Methuen (1892).

Green, F. E., *The Tyranny of the Countryside*, T. Fisher Unwin (1913).

Gyfford, Edward, *Designs for Elegant Cottages and Small Villas*, London (1806).

Haggard, H. Rider, *A Farmer's Year*, Longman (1899).

Haggard, H. Rider, *Rural England*, Longman (1902).

Hale, Thomas, *A Compleat Body of Husbandry* (1758).

Hammond, J. L. and B., *The Village Labourer*, Longman, Green (1913).

Hanawalt, Barbara A., *The Ties That Bound: Peasant Families in Medieval England*, Oxford University Press (1986).

Harper, Charles, *The Autocar Road Book*, Methuen (1910).

Harrison, W., *The Description of England* - see Furnivall, F. J.

Hartley, Dorothy, *Food in England*, Macdonald (1962).

Harvey, Nigel, *A History of Farm Buildings in England and Wales*, David & Charles (1970).

Havinden, Michael, 'The Model Village', in G. E. Mingay (ed.), *The Victorian Countryside*, Routledge & Kegan Paul (1981).

Heath, F. G., *British Rural Life and Labour* (1911).

Heath, F. G., *Peasant Life in the West of England*, 2nd edn., Sampson Low (1880).

Heath, F. G., *The English Peasantry* (1874).

Hill, Octavia, *Our Common Land*, Macmillan (1877).

Hoskins, W. G., *The Making of the English Landscape*, London (1955).

Hoskins, W. G., *The English Peasant*, Macmillan (1957).

Howe, J. A., *Geology of Building Stones*, Edward Arnold (1910).

Howitt, William, *The Rural Life of England*, Longman (1838).

Howkins, Alun, 'In the Sweat of thy Face: The Labourer and Work', in G. E. Mingay (ed.), *The Victorian Countryside*, Routledge & Kegan Paul (1981).

Huish, Marcus B., *The Happy England of Helen Allingham*, Adam and Charles Black (1903).

Hussey, Christopher, *The Life of Sir Edwin Lutyens*, London (1950).

Innocent, C. F., *The Development of English Building Construction*, Cambridge (1916).

Jefferies, Richard, *Hodge and his Masters*, Smith, Elder (1880).

Jekyll, Gertrude, *Colour Schemes for the Flower Garden*, 8th edn., Country Life (1936).

Jekyll, Gertrude, *Old English Household Life*, Batsford (1925).

Jekyll, Gertrude, *Old West Surrey*, Longmans, Green & Co. (1904).

Joad, C. E. M., *The Untutored Townsman's Invasion of the Country*, Faber & Faber (1946).

Kay, Joseph, *Free Trade in Land*, 4th edn., C. K. Paul (1879).

Keen, Maurice, *English Society in the Later Middle Ages 1348-1500*, Penguin (1990).

Kent, Nathaniel, *Hints to Gentlemen of Landed Property*, London (1775).

Knight, Richard Payne, *An Analytical Inquiry into the Principles of Taste*, 2nd edn., London (1805).

Knight, Richard Payne, *The Landscape: a Didactic Poem in Three Books*, 2nd edn., London (1795).

Knoop, Douglas & Jones, J. P., *The Medieval Mason*, Manchester University Press (1949).

Lancaster, Osbert, *Drayneflete Revealed*, John Murray (1949).

Lander, Hugh, and Rauter, Peter, *English Cottage Interiors*, Weidenfeld & Nicolson (1989).

Langland, William, Piers Plowman, ed. W. W. Skeat, Oxford (1886).

Laugier, *An Essay on Architecture*, London (1755).

Lethaby, W. R., *Philip Webb and His Work*,

Oxford University Press (1935).

Levine, D., *Family Formation in an Age of Nascent Capitalism*, Academic Press (1979).

Lindsay, Seymour, *Iron and Brass Implements of the English House*, Alec Tiranti (1964).

Loudon, John Claudius, *A Treatise on Forming, Improving and Managing Country Residences*, London (1806).

Loudon, John Claudius, *Encyclopaedia of Cottage, Farm, and Villa Architecture and Furniture*, London (1842).

Loudon, John Claudius, Suburban Gardener and Villa Companion, London (1838).

Lugar, Robert, *Architectural Sketches for Cottages, Rural Dwellings, and Villas*, London (1805).

Lugar, Robert, *The Country Gentleman's Architect*, London (1807).

Lyall, Sutherland, *Dream Cottages: From Cottage Ornée to Stockbroker Tudor*, Hale (1988).

Mackay, Alexander, Report on Rural Housing Conditions, *Morning Chronicle*, 24 October 1849.

Mais, S. P. B., *Let's Get Out Here*, Southern Railway (1937).

Malton, James, *An Essay on British Cottage Architecture*, London (1798).

Markham, Gervase, *The English House-wife* (1675).

Marsh, Jan, *Back to the Land*, Quartet (1982).

Marshall, J. D., *The Old Poor Law 1795 to 1850*, Macmillan (1985).

Mills, D. R. (ed.), *English Rural Communities: The Impact of a Specialised Economy*, Macmillan (1973).

Mingay, G. E., *Rural Life in Victorian England*, Sutton (1990).

Moseley, Malcolm J., 'The Rural Areas', in Gardiner, Vince and R. J. Johnston, *The Changing Geography of the United Kingdom*, 2nd edn., Routledge (1991).

Muthesius, Hermann, *The English House* (Das englische Haus), BSP (1987).

Oliver, Basil, *The Cottages of England: a Review of Their Types and Features From the Sixteenth to the Eighteenth Centuries*, Batsford (1929).

Orwin, C. S., *Problems of the Countryside*, Cambridge University Press (1945).

Ould, E. A. and J. Parkinson, *Old Cottages, Farm Houses, and Other Half-Timber Buildings in Shropshire, Herefordshire and Cheshire*, Batsford (1904).

Papworth, John Buonarotti, *Rural Residences*, London (1818).

Parker, Rowland, *The Common Stream*, Granada (1975).

Parry, M. L., 'The Changing Use of Land', in Gardiner, Vince and R. J. Johnston, *The Changing Geography of the United Kingdom*, 2nd edn., Routledge (1991).

Paston-Williams, Sara, *The Art of Dining: A History of Cooking and Eating*, The National Trust (1993).

Perry, P. J., 'Edward Girdlestone 1805-84: The Forgotten Evangelical', *Journal of Religious History*, IX, 3 (1977).

Perry, P. J., *British Farming in the Great Depression, 1870-1914*, David & Charles (1974).

Pevsner, Nikolaus (ed.), *The Buildings of England* series, Penguin (various dates).

Pevsner, Nikolaus, *Pioneers of Modern Design from William Morris to Walter Gropius*, Penguin (1984).

Philips, Randal, *The £1,000 House*, Country Life (1928).

Phythian-Adams, 'Rural Culture', in G. E. Mingay (ed.), *The Victorian Country-side*, Routledge & Kegan Paul (1981).

Plaw, John, *Rural Architecture: or Designs from the Simple Cottage to the Decorated Villa*, London (1802).

Plomer, W. (ed.), Kilvert's Diary 1870-1879: *Selections from the Diary of the Rev. Francis Kilvert*, Jonathan Cape (1964).

Pocock, Wiliam Fuller, *Architectural Designs for Rustic Cottages, Picturesque Dwellings, Villas, etc.*, London (1807).

Poor Law Commission: first report (1835); *second report* (1836).

Postan, M. M., 'Some Economic Evidence of Declining Population in the Later Middle Ages', *Economic History Review*, 2nd series, 2 (1950).

Price, Uvedale, *Essays on the Picturesque*, London (1810).

Prizeman, John, *Your House: the Outside View*, Hutchinson (1975).

Reyce, Robert, *A Breviary of Suffolk* (1618).

Richardson, Isabel, 'Vernacular Buildings Survey in Devon', *Views*, 21 (1994).

Richardson, Margaret, *Architects of the Arts and Crafts Movement*, Trefoil (1983).

Robinson, William, *The Wild Garden*, The Garden Office (1881).

Rowley, Trevor, *The High Middle Ages 1200-1550*, Paladin (1988).

Royal Commission on Employment of Children, Young Persons and Women in Agriculture: first report (1867-8); *second report* (1868-9); *third and fourth reports* (1870).

Royal Commission on Employment of Women and Children in Agriculture: Reports of Special Assistant Poor Law Commissioners (1843).

Royal Commission on Labour: the Agricultural Labourer, general report (1893-4).

Royal Commission on Poor Laws, Evidence from Rural Centres (1910).

Royal Commission on the Housing of the Working Classes, Minutes of Evidence (1884-5).

Rule, J. G., *Albion's People: English Society 1714-1815*, Longman (1992).

Rule, J. G., *The Labouring Classes in Early Industrial England, 1750-1850*, Longman (1986).

Rule, J. G., *The Vital Century: England's Developing Economy 1714-1815*, Longman (1992).

Rykwert, Joseph, 'Architecture', in Ford, Boris (ed.), *Modern Britain*, Cambridge University Press (1992).

Saint, Andrew, 'New Towns', in Ford, Boris (ed.), *Modern Britain*, Cambridge University Press (1992).

Saint, Andrew, *Richard Norman Shaw*, Yale (1976).

Salzman, L. F., *Building in England Down to 1540*, Oxford University Press (1952).

Scott, George Gilbert, *Remarks on Secular and Domestic Architecture*, John Murray (1857).

Sharpe, J. A., *Early Modern England: a Social History 1550-1760*, Edward Arnold (1987).

Shaw, Gwen and Shaw, Roy, 'The Cultural and Social Setting', in Ford, Boris (ed.), *Modern Britain*, Cambridge University Press (1992).

Simon, Sir John, *Public Health Reports*, ed. E. Seaton (1887).

Smith, Henry Herbert, *The Principles of Landed Estate Management*, Edward Arnold (1898).

Steer, Francis W., *Farm and Cottage Inventories of Mid-Essex 1635-1749*, 2nd edn., Phillimore (1969).

Stenton, Doris Mary, *English Society in the Early Middle Ages*, Pelican (1951).

Stone, Lawrence and Stone, Jeanne C. Fawtier, *An Open Elite? England 1540-1880*, Oxford (1986).

Stone, Lawrence, *The Crisis of the Aristocracy*, Clarendon (1965).

Stone, Lawrence, *The Family, Sex and Marriage in England 1500-1800*, Weidenfeld & Nicolson (1977).

Storch, R. W., *Popular Culture and Custom in Nineteenth-century England*, Croom Helm (1982).

Sykes, Frank, *This Farming Business*, Faber and Faber (1944).

Thompson, E. P., *The Making of the English Working Class*, Penguin (1968).

Thompson, F. M. L., *English Landed Society in the Nineteenth Century*, Routledge & Kegan Paul (1963).

Thompson, F. M. L., 'Landowners and the Rural Community', in G. E. Mingay (ed.), *The Victorian Countryside*, Routledge & Kegan Paul (1981).

Thomson, David, *England in the Nineteenth Century*, Penguin (1978).

Turner, M. E., *Enclosures in Britain 1750-1830*, Macmillan (1984).

Warner, Richard, *Tour through the Northern Counties* (1812).

Weaver, Lawrence, *The 'Country Life' Book of Cottages*, Country Life (1913).

Weaver, Lawrence, *Cottages: their Planning, Design and Materials*, Country Life (1926).

White, Charles, *Country Walks* (1st, 2nd and 3rd series), London Transport (1936-9).

White, Gilbert, *The Natural History of Selborne*, George Routledge (1905).

Wiliams-Ellis, Clough, *England and the Octopus*, Geoffrey Bles (1928).

Williams, Alfred, *Villages of the White Horse* (1913).

Wood, John, *A Series of Plans for Cottages or Habitations of the Labourer*, London (1781).

Wood, Margaret, *The English Medieval House*, Bracken Books (1985).

Wood, Michael, *Domesday: Search for the Roots of England*, British Broadcasting Corp.(1990).

Woodforde, John, *The Truth about Cottages*, Routledge and Kegan Paul (1979).

Wright, L., *Clean and Decent: The Fascinating History of the Bathroom and the Water Closet*, Routledge (1960).

Young, Arthur, *General View of the Agriculture of Norfolk*, Board of Agriculture (1804).

Index

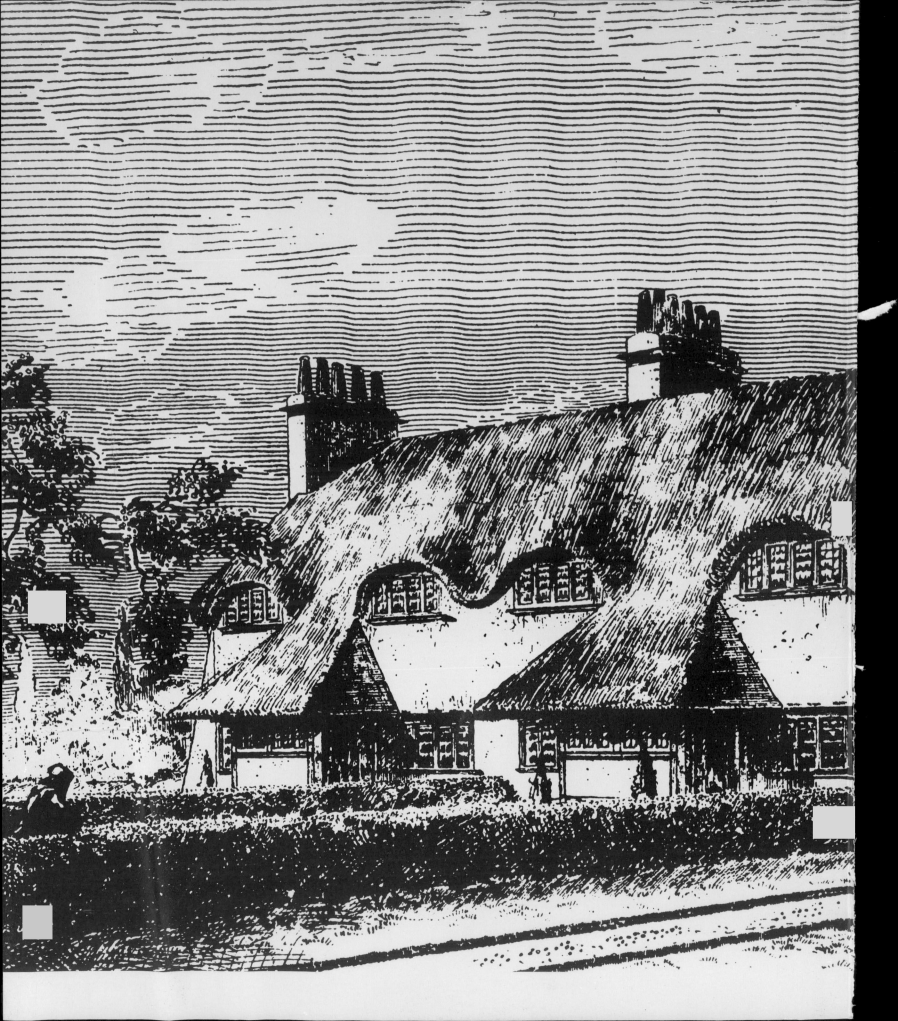